THE CANONS OF
JIHAD

TERRORISTS' STRATEGY FOR DEFEATING AMERICA

Edited by Jim Lacey

NAVAL
Ann

Naval Institute Press
291 Wood Road
Annapolis, MD 21402

Library of Congress Cataloging-in-Publication Data
The canons of jihad : terrorists' strategy for defeating America
/ edited by Jim Lacey.
    p. cm.
Includes bibliographical references and index.
ISBN 978-1-59114-461-8 (alk. paper)
    1. Terrorism—History—Sources.   2. Jihad—History—
Sources. 3. Anti-Americanism—Islamic countries—Sources.
4. Islamic fundamentalism. 5. Islam and politics. I. Lacey, Jim,
1958– II. Title: Terrorist's strategy for defeating America.
HV6431.C353 2008
363.325—dc22
                                    2007046136

Printed in the United States of America on acid-free paper

14 13 12 11 10 09 08   9 8 7 6 5 4 3 2
First printing

Contents

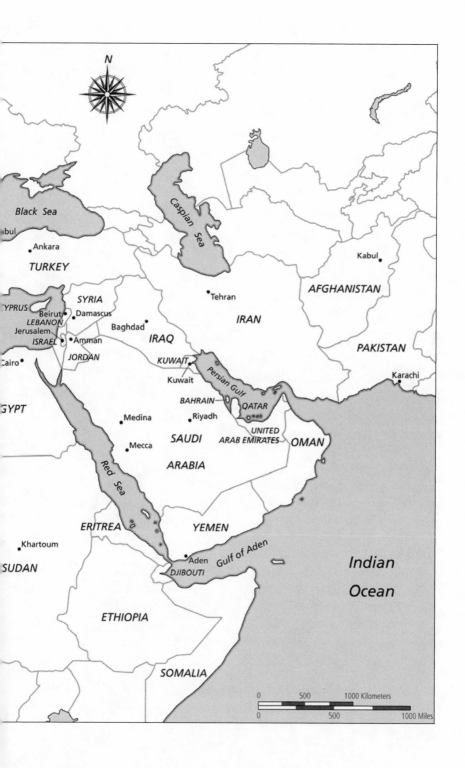

N

Black Sea

Caspian Sea

bul

Ankara

Kabul

TURKEY

AFGHANISTAN

CYPRUS   SYRIA

Tehran

YPRUS   Beirut   Damascus

IRAN

PAKISTAN

LEBANON

Jerusalem

Baghdad

ISRAEL   Amman

IRAQ

Karachi

Cairo

JORDAN

KUWAIT

Persian Gulf

EGYPT

Kuwait

BAHRAIN

QATAR

Medina

Riyadh

UNITED

SAUDI

ARAB EMIRATES

OMAN

Mecca

ARABIA

Red Sea

ERITREA

YEMEN

Gulf of Aden

Khartoum

Aden

Indian

SUDAN

DJIBOUTI

Ocean

ETHIOPIA

SOMALIA

0   500   1000 Kilometers

0   500   1000 Miles

Introduction

Since the terrorist attack of 9/11 several compilations of the statements of jihadists and their organizations have been published. Such compilations provide value, as they help Westerners understand some of the motivations of the jihad movement. However, they all suffer from a major defect. These collections consist of statements the jihadists wish to tell us about themselves, and as such they are of limited value in helping us understand the underlying dogmas that propel their destructive and nihilistic movement.

Analysts have long understood that the best way to understand jihadists is to look at what they say to each other. Yet even though many of the most important works of the jihadist movement have been translated, only a very few analysts (and virtually no interested layperson) have bothered to read them. The reason for this is simple: These works are incredibly dense reading. First, many of the works are poorly constructed and meander back and forth over a myriad of topics. This problem is further aggravated by the fact that most of the jihadist thinkers, although well versed in the Qur'an, have absolutely no concept of economics, international diplomacy, or anything else that makes the modern world run. For a knowledgeable Westerner, reading jihadist commentary on international finance is a painful experience.

But what stops most Western readers dead in their tracks is the overwhelming amount of religious or quasi-religious scholarship found in all of these texts. It is not enough for a jihadist author to declare, "Jihad is an individual obligation of every Muslim." He must then follow that statement, and all his other statements, with every quote from the Qur'an that supports his viewpoint. Moreover, these authors feel a need to go further and present dozens of quotes from each medieval Islamic scholar who even tangentially touched upon the topic at hand. In the end every ten pages of jihadist dogma ends up buried under a hundred pages of religious and quasi-religious justification.

What is needed is a collection that cuts through most of what makes the jihadist canon unreadable to a broader Western audience. Therefore, in order to get to the essence of jihadists' beliefs, I have removed most of the thousands of religious justifications in these documents, along with many of the ubiquitous recountings of Islamic and Western history. Only those quotes and historical comments absolutely necessary to understanding the text have been retained.

The premise behind this work is that if we want to understand our enemy, it is essential to capture the important strands of their beliefs. Dragging the average reader, or even the professional analyst, through fourteen hundred years' worth of selected quotes from often obscure Islamic scholars is much less critical. Some may argue that a true understanding of the jihadist mindset can only be gained by reading these justifications and thereby developing a deeper understanding of why they believe what they do. This may be true if you are a scholar studying the jihadist movement for academic reasons. But after reading through thousands of pages of these justifications, before stripping them out, I can attest to the fact that there are precious few additional insights into the jihadist mindset to be gained by wading through them. For those who insist on trying, each of the works in this book is available in its entirety from various sources— except for the al-Suri essay at the end of this book. (See chap. 10)

The al-Suri document is actually excerpted from his much longer work, *Call to Global Islamic Resistance*, which has been called the most important strategic document to be produced by al Qaida or any jihadist organization in over a decade. Unfortunately, it is 1,600 pages long, and three-quarters of it consists of al-Suri's version of world history and almost incomprehensible Islamic scholarship. A committed jihadist, steeped in religious dogma, might be able to handle it, but for most of us it is impenetrable. Separately, I reduced the complete al-Suri manifesto to its bare essence.

When I took several copies of this reduced work to a conference the Central Intelligence Agency was running on al-Suri, the CIA analysts present told me that this was exactly what they needed. When a more senior CIA analyst told them that the entire translated document was available for them to look at on a CIA-sponsored Web site, one of the analysts responded, "No one has time to go through the whole document. We just need the important stuff out of it." With that endorsement, and the encouragement of some scholars at the conference, I am publishing the condensed version of al-Suri's manifesto separately (*A Terrorist's Call to Global Jihad*, Naval Institute Press, 2008). For those who may read only this book, however, I have included some of his more interesting thoughts.

Because there is so much jihadist literature from which to choose, some may quibble with the works selected for inclusion in this book. The works were recommended by a number of experts at the Institute for Defense Analyses who for the past year have been conducting the Terrorist Perspective Project. This fascinating project, run by Mark Stout and Mike Pease, is an effort to get past the mirror-imaging problem that plagues much intelligence analysis by studying the jihad movement in light of what they say to themselves and think about themselves. Rather than trying to guess at terrorists' motivations from our Western viewpoint, this team has been looking at the jihad movement through the jihadists' own eyes. When I asked them what documents and thinkers have had and continue to have the most impact on the movement, they recommended the works included in this book. After gathering my initial list of works, I checked it with the experts at the Combating Terrorism Center at West Point and found they were in agreement with my selection.

What follows is a collection of the writings that intellectually underpins the jihadist movement. Starting with the founder and a leading early member of the Muslim Brotherhood, Hasan al-Banna and Al Shaheed Sayyid Qutb, the reader will discover the basis of the jihad movement, which calls the entire Islamic world to jihad against the "oppressors." What is most notable about these and most other early jihad writers is their focus on what they call the "near enemy"—their own governments, which they consider unjust and apostate. It was not until Osama bin Laden appeared and came under the influence of later writers, such as Sheikh Abdullah 'Azzam, that the jihadists focused their attentions on the "far enemy"—the United States. Their rationale for this switch was that although the most important task remained the removal of their own apostate rulers, this would not happen as long as the United States was supporting them militarily and financially. So in order to bring about regime change at home, it became imperative to destroy the United States.

By following the recommendations of writers such as 'Azzam, Muhammad al-Salam Faraj, and General S. K. Malik, the jihadists built an organization they thought would lead to an Islamic reawakening that would throw off the yoke of oppression and be able to defeat the United States. They were greatly encouraged in this outlook by the overthrow of the Soviet empire, which their writings credit entirely to the courage of the mujahideen in Afghanistan, belittling any contributions the United States and NATO made to that outcome. In their writings it becomes clear that they consider the Soviet Union the greatest military power the world had ever known, and to their way of thinking, if they could beat the Soviets, the United States would be even easier prey.

The American reaction to 9/11 ended that presumption. As al-Suri makes clear, the jihadists did not expect and were not prepared for the violent assaults the United States unleashed on their global infrastructure. According to al-Suri and other writers, the jihadist cadres were virtually annihilated by the U.S. response, and since then al-Suri and other strategists have been looking for new concepts and strategies on how to conduct the next phase of the jihad. As these destroyed cadres begin to rebuild themselves, jihadists are once again turning to their original thinkers to find justification for their actions. This volume is presented in the hope that through a more thorough understanding of the motivating voices of jihad, we will be able to both destroy these enemies and protect ourselves from them.

CHAPTER 1
Jihad against Jews and Crusaders

ISSUED BY THE WORLD ISLAMIC FRONT, FEBRUARY 23, 1998

Editor's Note: Most people missed Osama bin Laden's declaration of war against the United States, issued three years before 9/11. It is produced here in its entirety and presents a unique view into our enemy's outlook and determination.

Praise be to God, who revealed the Book, controls the clouds, defeats factionalism, and says in his Book: "But when the forbidden months are past, then fight and slay the pagans wherever ye find them, seize them, beleaguer them, and lie in wait for them in every stratagem (of war)"; and peace be upon our Prophet, Muhammad Bin-'Abdallah, who said, "I have been sent with the sword between my hands to ensure that no one but God is worshiped, God who put my livelihood under the shadow of my spear and who inflicts humiliation and scorn on those who disobey my orders."

The Arabian Peninsula has never—since God made it flat, created its desert, and encircled it with seas—been stormed by any forces like the crusader armies spreading in it like locusts, eating its riches, and wiping out its plantations. All this is happening at a time in which nations are attacking Muslims like people fighting over a plate of food. In the light of the grave situation and the lack of support, you and we are obliged to discuss current events, and we should all agree on how to settle the matter.

No one argues today about three facts that are known to everyone; we will list them in order to remind everyone:

- First, for over seven years the United States has been occupying the lands of Islam in the holiest of places, the Arabian Peninsula, plundering its riches, dictating to its rulers, humiliating its people, terrorizing its neighbors, and turning its bases in the peninsula into a spearhead through which to fight the neighboring Muslim peoples. If some people have in the past argued about the fact of the occupation, all the people of the Peninsula have now acknowledged it. The best proof of this is the Americans' continuing aggression against the Iraqi people using the peninsula as a staging post, even though all its rulers are against their territories being used to that end, but they are helpless.
- Second, despite the great devastation inflicted on the Iraqi people by the crusader-Zionist alliance, and despite the huge number of those killed, which has exceeded one million—despite all this, the Americans are once again trying to repeat the horrific massacres, as though they are not content with the protracted blockade imposed after the ferocious war or the fragmentation and devastation. So here they come to annihilate what is left of this people and to humiliate their Muslim neighbors.
- Third, if the Americans' aims behind these wars are religious and economic, the aim is also to serve the Jews' petty state and divert attention from its occupation of Jerusalem and murder of Muslims there. The best proof of this is their eagerness to destroy Iraq, the strongest neighboring Arab state, and their endeavor to fragment all the states of the region, such as Iraq, Saudi Arabia, Egypt, and Sudan, into paper "statelets" and through their disunion and weakness to guarantee Israel's survival and the continuation of the brutal crusade occupation of the peninsula.

All these crimes and sins committed by the Americans are a clear declaration of war on God, his messenger, and Muslims. And *ulema* [Muslim legal scholars] have throughout Islamic history unanimously agreed that the jihad is an individual duty if the enemy destroys the Muslim countries. This was revealed by Imam Bin-Qadamah in "Al-Mughni," Imam al-Kisa'i in "Al-Bada'i," al-Qurtubi in his interpretation, and the sheikh of al-Islam in his books, where he said: "As for the fighting to repulse an enemy, it is aimed at defending sanctity and religion, and it is a duty as agreed by the *ulema*. Nothing is more sacred than belief except repulsing an enemy who is attacking religion and life." On that basis, and in compliance with

God's order, we issue the following fatwa to all Muslims: The ruling to kill the Americans and their allies—civilians and military—is an individual duty for every Muslim who can do it in any country in which it is possible to do it, in order to liberate the al-Aqsa Mosque and the holy mosque [Mecca] from their grip, and in order for their armies to move out of all the lands of Islam, defeated and unable to threaten any Muslim. This is in accordance with the words of Almighty God: "and fight the pagans all together as they fight you all together" and "fight them until there is no more tumult or oppression, and there prevail justice and faith in God." This is in addition to the words of Almighty God: "And why should ye not fight in the cause of God and of those who, being weak, are ill-treated (and oppressed)?—women and children, whose cry is: 'Our Lord, rescue us from this town, whose people are oppressors; and raise for us from thee one who will help!'" We, with God's help, call on every Muslim who believes in God and wishes to be rewarded to comply with God's order to kill the Americans and plunder their money wherever and whenever they find it. We also call on Muslim *ulema*, leaders, youths, and soldiers to launch the raid on Satan's U.S. troops and the devil's supporters allying with them, and to displace those who are behind them so that they may learn a lesson. Almighty God said: "O ye who believe, give your response to God and his Apostle, when he calleth you to that which will give you life. And know that God cometh between a man and his heart, and that it is he to whom ye shall all be gathered." Almighty God also says: "O ye who believe, what is the matter with you, that when ye are asked to go forth in the cause of God, ye cling so heavily to the earth! Do ye prefer the life of this world to the hereafter? But little is the comfort of this life, as compared with the here- after. Unless ye go forth, he will punish you with a grievous penalty, and put others in your place; but him ye would not harm in the least. For God hath power over all things." Almighty God also says: "So lose no heart, nor fall into despair. For ye must gain mastery if ye are true in faith."

Signatories: SHEIKH OSAMA BIN MUHAMMAD BIN LADEN; AYMAN AL-ZAWAHIRI, AMIR OF THE JIHAD GROUP IN EGYPT; ABU-YASIR RIFA'I AHMAD TAHA, EGYPTIAN ISLAMIC GROUP; SHEIKH MIR HAMZAH, SECRETARY OF THE JAMIAT-UL-ULEMA-E-PAKISTAN; AND FAZLUR RAHMAN, AMIR OF THE JIHAD MOVEMENT IN BANGLADESH

CHAPTER 2
Jihad

HASAN AL-BANNA

Hasan al-Banna was the founder of the Muslim Brotherhood in 1928. The Brotherhood was the first mass-based, overtly political movement to oppose the rising tide of Western ideas in the Middle East. The organization saw these ideas as the root of decay in the Muslim world and advocated a return to the pure Islam of the Prophet's times. Under al-Banna's guidance the Brotherhood saw spectacular growth throughout the 1930s and 1940s. As it expanded, it quickly shifted from advocating moral reform to becoming directly active in Egyptian politics. During this time radical tendencies grew within the movement and al-Banna established a "secret apparatus" (al-jihaz al-sirri) within the organization that carried out a number of assassinations against the Brotherhood's perceived enemies. Al-Banna himself was assassinated in 1949 in the Egyptian's government's retaliation for the Brotherhood's assassination of the Egyptian prime minister, Nuqrashi Pasha. Before he died, however, he published Jihad, *which continues to inspire today's Islamic radicals.*

Preface

The Muslim world today is faced with tyranny and injustice. Indeed, oppression and hardship is not just limited to the Muslim world; rather, many non-Muslim states are subject to oppression at the hands of the world's leading military and economic powers. Islam has allowed jihad as a means to prevent oppression, yet Muslims have forgotten this for too long.

4

Though jihad may only be a part of the answer to the problems of the *ummah* [community of believers], it is an extremely important part. Jihad is to offer ourselves to Allah for his cause. Indeed, every person should according to Islam prepare himself/herself for jihad, and every person should eagerly and patiently wait for the day when Allah will call them to show their willingness to sacrifice their lives. We should all ask ourselves, Is there a quicker way to heaven? It is with this in mind that this booklet is being published.

Our situation today requires action on all fronts. Everybody has a role to play in today's great jigsaw—those who are attempting to establish the Islamic state have to continue doing so, focusing their minds onto such a project, those who are faced with tyranny at the hands of neighboring armies have to defend themselves with their lives, and those that have the opportunity of giving Islam to the world should do so.

This is an important booklet for three reasons. First, it deals with an important issue—that of jihad. Second, it is important because it has been written by one of the most prominent mujahideen of this century, Imam Hasan al-Banna. And third, it is important because it deals with an issue that the *ummah* seems to have misunderstood or forgotten. Imam Hasan al-Banna is the founder of the Muslim Brotherhood and one of the pioneers of today's Islamic revival. It is the right of the contemporary Muslim generation that they should have access to the writings of this great reformer; especially on this important topic.

The imam, may Allah bless him, shows us that ultimately only Islam can save mankind from itself. And jihad on the individual and international scale will be a necessary part of this process of change.

DR. A. M. A. FAHMY
INTERNATIONAL ISLAMIC FORUM

All Muslims Must Make Jihad

Jihad is an obligation from Allah on every Muslim and cannot be ignored or evaded. Allah has ascribed great importance to jihad and has made the reward of the martyrs and the fighters a splendid one. Only those who have acted similarly and who have modeled themselves upon the martyrs in their performance of jihad can join them in this reward. Furthermore, Allah has specifically honored the mujahideen with certain exceptional qualities, both spiritual and practical, to benefit them in this world and the next. Their pure blood is a symbol of victory in this world and the mark of success and felicity in the world to come.

Those who can only find excuses, however, have been warned of extremely dreadful punishments, and Allah has described them with the most unfortunate of names. He has reprimanded them for their cowardice and lack of spirit, and castigated them for their weakness and truancy. In this world, they will be surrounded by dishonor, and in the next they will be surrounded by the fire from which they shall not escape though they may possess much wealth. The weaknesses of abstention and evasion of jihad are regarded by Allah as one of the major sins, and one of the seven sins that guarantee failure.

Islam is concerned with the question of jihad and the mobilization of the entire *ummah* into one body to defend the cause with all its strength. The verses of the Qur'an and the Sunnah of Muhammad are overflowing with noble ideals and they summon the people to jihad, to warfare, to the armed forces, and to all means of land and sea fighting. Clarifications are not required.

The Qur'an on Jihad

Jihad is ordained for you (Muslims) though you dislike it, and it may be that you dislike something that is good for you and that you like something that is bad for you. Allah knows but you do not know. (Surat al-Baqarah [2], ayah 216) [Qur'an]

Think not of those who are killed in the Way of Allah as dead. Nay, they are alive, with their Lord, and they have provision. They rejoice in what Allah has bestowed upon them of his Bounty, rejoicing for the sake of those who have not yet joined them, but are left behind (not yet martyred) that on them no fear shall come, nor shall they grieve. (Surat al-Imran [3], ayah 169–70)

Let those (believers) who sell the life of this world for the Hereafter fight in the cause of Allah, and whosoever fights in the Cause of Allah, and is killed or is victorious, We shall bestow on him a great reward. (Surat an-Nisaa' [4], ayah 74)

Allah urges Muslims to remain alert and to acquire experience in warfare, in armies and troops, or as individuals, as circumstances may dictate. Allah also reprimands those who are slack, cowards, or opportunists. Notice how Allah associates warfare with prayer and fasting, establishing it as one of the pillars of Islam. And how he refutes the false arguments of the waverers, and encourages those who are scared to the utmost degree to plunge into battle and to face death unflinchingly and bravely, showing them that they will welcome death, and that if they die in jihad, they will receive the most magnificent recompense for their lives, and that they will not lose any of their contribution or sacrifice, however small.

And his words concerning fighting with People of the Book [Christians and Jews]:

> Fight against those who believe not in Allah, nor in the Last Day, nor forbid that which has been forbidden by Allah and his Messenger and those who acknowledge not the Religion of Truth [Islam], from among the People of the Book, until they pay the *jizya* [tax levied on non-Muslim men in lieu of military service] with willing submission, and feel themselves subdued. (Surat at-Tawbah [9], ayah 29)

These, brother, are some examples of the Qur'anic references on jihad. Its virtues are made clear, and those who do jihad are given the good news of the magnificent reward that will be waiting for them. The Book of Allah is filled with examples like these, and anyone who reads the Qur'an and pays attention to its meaning will be astounded at the negligence of Muslims who have failed to take advantage of this reward.

The Scholars on Jihad

I would like to present to you some of the opinions from jurisprudence of the Islamic schools of thought, including some latter-day authorities regarding the rules of jihad and the necessity for preparedness. From this we will come to realize how far the *ummah* has deviated in its practice of Islam, as can be seen from the consensus of its scholars on the question of jihad.

The author of the *Majma' al-Anhar fi Sharh Multaqal-Abhar*, in describing the rules of jihad according to the Hanafi school, said: "Jihad linguistically means to exert one's utmost effort in fighting the unbelievers, and involves all possible efforts that are necessary to dismantle the power of the enemies of Islam including beating them, plundering their wealth, destroying their places of worship and smashing their idols. This means that jihad is to strive to the utmost to ensure the strength of Islam by such means as fighting those who fight you and the *dhimmies* [Christians and Jews who submit to the rule of Islam and pay a special tax] and the apostates (who are the worst of unbelievers, for they disbelieved after they have affirmed their belief).

It is obligatory to fight with the enemies. The imam must send a military expedition to the Dar al-Harb [literally, "Land of War," but actually referring to any area not controlled by Islam] at least once or twice every year, and the people must support him in this. If some of the people fulfill the obligation, the remainder are released from the obligation. If this communal obligation cannot be fulfilled by that group, then the responsibility lies with the closest adjacent group, and then the closest after that, etc., and if it cannot be fulfilled except by all the people, it then becomes an individual obligation on everyone.

And Ibn Qudama of the Hanbali school, said, Jihad is an obligation.

If two armies meet and two lines of soldiers confront one another, those present are forbidden to leave the battlefield, and it becomes an obligation on each one to remain at his station. If the imam calls a group of people to arms, then they must join his military forces. And he should at least announce jihad once every year.

Imam Ahmad bin Hanbal said: "I know of nothing after the divine commandments more excellent than jihad, and campaigning by sea is more excellent than campaigning on land."

And it says in *Al-Muhalla* of Ibn Hazm: "Jihad is obligatory on Muslims, but if the borders of Muslims can be protected, the enemy can be repelled and fought within his own territory then the remainder of the people are released from it. And if not, then the obligation remains."

The scholarly people are of one opinion on this matter, as should be evident. They all agreed unanimously that jihad is an obligation imposed upon the Islamic *ummah* in order to spread Islam, and that jihad is an obligation if an enemy attacks Muslim lands. Today, my brother, the Muslims, as you know, are forced to be subservient before others and are ruled by disbelievers. Our lands have been besieged, and our personal possessions, respect, honor, dignity, and privacy violated. Yet still Muslims fail to fulfill the responsibility of jihad that is on their shoulders. Hence in this situation it becomes the duty of each and every Muslim to make jihad. He should prepare himself mentally and physically such that when comes the decision of Allah, he will be ready.

Why Do the Muslims Fight?

People have for some time now ridiculed this, but today these same people acknowledge that preparation for war is the surest way to peace! Allah did not ordain jihad for Muslims so that it may be used as a tool of oppression or tyranny or so that it may be used by some to further their personal gains. Rather, jihad is used to safeguard the mission of spreading Islam. For Islam, even as it ordains jihad, extols peace.

Muslims in war had only one concern and this was to make the name of Allah supreme; there was no room at all for any other objective. The wish for glory and reputation were forbidden to Muslims. The love of wealth, the misappropriation of the benefits of war, and striving to conquer through unjust methods are all made forbidden to the Muslim. Only one intention was possible, and that was the offering of sacrifice and the taking of pains for the guidance of mankind.

Mohammad's companions' behavior in battle and in the territories they conquered indicates the extent to which they abstained from indulging in their personal desires and cravings, and the extent of their dedication to their fundamental and original goal: the guidance of mankind to the truth of Allah's word. The charge of some people who accuse the companions of being covetous of power and authority, desirous of grabbing countries and ascendancy, or that a passion for earning a living was driving their activities is ludicrous. [Editor's note: Though the charge does seem historically accurate.]

Mercy in the Islamic Jihad

The Islamic jihad is the noblest of endeavors, and its method of realization is the most sublime and exalted. For Allah has forbidden aggression. Allah instructs the Muslims to act with the utmost mercy. For when they fight, they do not instigate hostilities, nor do they steal nor plunder property, nor do they violate someone's honor, nor do they indulge in wanton destruction. In their warfare they are the best of fighters, just as in peace they are the most excellent of peacemakers.

It is forbidden to slay women, children, and old people, to kill the wounded, or to disturb monks, hermits, and the peaceful who offer no resistance. Contrast this mercy with the murderous warfare of the "civilized" people and their terrible atrocities! Compare their international law alongside this all-embracing, divinely ordained justice!

Associated Matters Concerning Jihad

Many Muslims today mistakenly believe that fighting the enemy is a lesser jihad and that fighting one's ego is a greater jihad. The following narration is quoted as proof: "We have returned from the lesser jihad to embark on the greater jihad." They said: "What is the greater jihad?" He said: "The jihad of the heart, or the jihad against one's ego."

This narration is used by some to lessen the importance of fighting, to discourage any preparation for combat, and to deter any offering of jihad in Allah's way. This narration is not a sound tradition. Nevertheless, even if it were a sound tradition, it would never warrant abandoning jihad or preparing for it in order to rescue the territories of Muslims and repel the attacks of the disbelievers. Let it be known that this narration simply emphasizes the importance of struggling against one's ego so that Allah will be the sole purpose of everyone's actions. Nothing compares to the honor of the supreme martyrdom or the reward that is waiting for the mujahideen.

Epilogue

My brothers! The *ummah* that knows how to die a noble and honorable death is granted an exalted life in this world and eternal felicity in the next. Degradation and dishonor are the results of the love of this world and the fear of death. Therefore prepare for jihad and be the lovers of death.

CHAPTER 3
Milestones

AL SHAHEED SAYYID QUTB

Sayyid Qutb was born in 1906 to a well-to-do farming family in Egypt. In his writings Sayyid Qutb attributed his strong bent toward religion to the influence of his mother, who inculcated a love for the Qur'an within him; she was determined that her children should all become *buffaz* (memorizers of the holy book).

Sayyid Qutb's earliest education was in the local village school, where by the age of ten he had memorized the Qur'an. In 1929 he entered Cairo University, where he earned a bachelor of arts degree in education. After graduation he became a college professor and then went on to join the Ministry of Education as inspector of schools.

Qutb's turning point came in 1949, when he went to the United States to study in educational administration. Over a two-year period he worked in several different institutions and traveled. His reaction to Western society was distinctly negative; he found it hopelessly materialistic, corrupt, and morally loose.

Even before he left for the United States, Qutb had taken an interest in the teachings of the Muslim Brotherhood, Egypt's leading Islamic group. Upon his return to Egypt, Qutb became one of the movement's leading intellectuals, and by the mid-1950s he was one of its leading figures. He became active in the Brotherhood's Bureau of Guidance and took charge of the office responsible for propagating Islamic views of society. In this role he became the intellectual leader of the Brotherhood, expressing his opinions in voluminous books and numerous journal articles.

After a 1954 attempt on the life of Egypt's President Nasser by the Brotherhood, the would-be assassin and six other Brotherhood members *were executed, thousands more were arrested, and the society was again declared illegal. Qutb was among those arrested and was sentenced to fifteen years' imprisonment. During his years in prison, lasting until mid-1964, he completed his influential commentary on the Qur'an (In the Shadow of the Qur'an) in eight volumes.*

After his release, Qutb continued to write and to work for the Islamic cause, until arrested again on the charge of attempting to overthrow the Egyptian government. The basis of the charge was his last book, Milestones, *which sanctioned force as a means to bring about an Islamic revolution and to transform society. In August 1966, Qutb was executed.* Milestones *has since become the ideological underpinning of the jihadist movement.*

Introduction

Mankind today is on the brink of a precipice, because humanity is devoid of those vital values that are necessary not only for its healthy development but also for its real progress. Even the Western world realizes that Western civilization is unable to present any healthy values for the guidance of mankind. It knows that it does not possess anything that will satisfy its own conscience and justify its existence.

It is essential for mankind to have new leadership!

The leadership of mankind by Western man is now on the decline, not because Western culture has become poor materially or because its economic and military power has become weak. The period of the Western system has come to an end primarily because it is deprived of those life-giving values that enabled it to be the leader of mankind.

It is necessary for the new leadership to preserve and develop the material fruits of the creative genius of Europe, and also to provide mankind with such high ideals and values as have so far remained undiscovered by mankind, and will also acquaint humanity with a way of life that is harmonious with human nature, which is positive and constructive, and that is practicable.

Islam is the only System that possesses these values and this way of life.

The period of the resurgence of science has also come to an end. This period, which began with the Renaissance in the sixteenth century after

Christ and reached its zenith in the eighteenth and nineteenth centuries, does not possess a reviving spirit.

All nationalistic and chauvinistic ideologies that have appeared in modern times, and all the movements and theories derived from them, have also lost their vitality. In short, all manmade individual or collective theories have proved to be failures.

At this crucial and bewildering juncture, the turn of Islam and the Muslim community has arrived—the turn of Islam, which does not prohibit material inventions.

If Islam is again to play the role of the leader of mankind, then it is necessary that the Muslim community be restored to its original form.

It is necessary to revive that Muslim community that is buried under the debris of the manmade traditions of several generations and is crushed under the weight of those false laws and customs that are not even remotely related to the Islamic teachings, and that, in spite of all this, calls itself the "world of Islam."

I am aware that between the attempt at "revival" and the attainment of "leadership" there is a great distance, as the Muslim community has long ago vanished and the leadership of mankind has long since passed to other ideologies and other nations. This was the era during which Europe's genius created its marvelous works in science, culture, law, and material production, due to which mankind has progressed to great heights of creativity and material comfort. It is not easy to find fault with the inventors of such marvelous things, especially since what we call the "world of Islam" is completely devoid of all this beauty.

But in spite of all this, it is necessary to revive Islam. The distance between the revival of Islam and the attainment of world leadership may be vast, and there may be great difficulties on the way, but the first step must be taken for the revival of Islam.

If we are to perform our task with insight and wisdom, we must first know clearly the nature of those qualities on the basis of which the Muslim community can fulfill its obligation as the leader of the world. This is essential so that we may not commit any blunders at the very first stage of its reconstruction and revival.

The Muslim community today is neither capable of nor required to present before mankind great genius in material inventions, which will make the world bow its head before its supremacy and thus reestablish once more its world leadership. Europe's creative mind is far ahead in this area, and at least for a few centuries to come we cannot expect to compete with Europe and attain supremacy over it in these fields. Hence we must have some other quality, that quality that modern civilization does not possess.

To attain the leadership of mankind, we must have something to offer besides material progress, and this other quality can only be a faith and a way of life that on the one hand conserves the benefits of modern science and technology and on the other fulfills the basic human needs on the same level of excellence as technology has fulfilled them in the sphere of material comfort. And then this faith and way of life must take concrete form in a human society—in other words, in a Muslim society.

If we look at the sources and foundations of modern ways of living, it becomes clear that the whole world is steeped in ignorance of the Divine guidance and all the marvelous material comforts and high-level inventions do not diminish this ignorance. It is based on rebellion against God's sovereignty on earth. It transfers to man one of the greatest attributes of God, namely, sovereignty, and makes some men lords over others. It takes the form of claiming that the right to create values, to legislate rules of collective behavior, and to choose any way of life rests with men, without regard to what God has prescribed. The result of this rebellion against the authority of God is the oppression of his creatures. Thus the humiliation of the common man under the Communist systems and the exploitation of individuals and nations due to greed for wealth and imperialism under the capitalist systems are but a corollary of rebellion against God's authority.

It is essential that our community arrange its affairs according to Islamic law and show it to the world. In order to bring this about, we need to initiate the movement of Islamic revival in some Muslim country. Only such a revivalist movement will eventually attain to the status of world leadership.

How is it possible to start the task of reviving Islam?

It is necessary that there should be a vanguard that sets out with this determination and then keeps walking on the path, marching through the vast ocean of ignorance that has encompassed the entire world. During its course, it should keep itself somewhat aloof from this all-encompassing ignorance and should also keep some ties with it.

It is necessary that this vanguard should know the landmarks and the milestones of the road toward this goal so that they may recognize the starting place, the nature, the responsibilities, and the ultimate purpose of this long journey.

The milestones will necessarily be determined by the light of the first source of this faith—the Holy Qur'an—and from its basic teachings, and from the concept that it created in the minds of the first group of Muslims.

I have written Milestones for this vanguard, which I consider to be a waiting reality about to be materialized.

The Unique Qur'anic Generation

The callers to Islam in every country and in every period should give thought to one particular aspect of the history of Islam, and they should ponder over it deeply. This is related to the method of inviting people to Islam and its ways of training.

At one time this message created a generation—the generation of the companions of the Prophet. After this, no other generation of this caliber was ever again to be found. The Qur'an is still in our hands, and the Hadith of the Prophet, which gives us his guidance in practical affairs, is also in our hands, as they were in the hands of the first Muslim community. God has taken the responsibility for preserving the Holy Qur'an on himself because he knows that Islam can be established and can benefit mankind even after the time of the Prophet. The spring from which the Companions of the Prophet drank was the Qur'an and Hadith of the Prophet, and his teachings were offspring of this fountainhead.

The Holy Qur'an was the only source from which they quenched their thirst, and this was the only mold in which they formed their lives. This was the only guidance for them, not because there was no civilization or culture or science or books or schools. Indeed, there was Roman culture, which even today is considered to be the foundation of European culture. There was the heritage of Greek culture—its logic, its philosophy, and its arts—which are still a source of inspiration for Western thought.

Thus we believe that this generation did not place sole reliance on the Book of God for the understanding of their religion because of any ignorance of civilization and culture, but it was all according to a well-thought-out plan and method.

This generation drank solely from this spring and thus attained a unique distinction in history. In later times other sources mingled with it, such as Greek philosophy and logic, ancient Persian legends and their ideas, Jewish scriptures and traditions, and Christian theology. Later generations

obtained their training from this mixed source, and hence the like of the
first generation never arose again. Thus we can say without any reservations that the main reason for the difference between the first group of
Muslims and later Muslims is that the purity of the first source of Islamic
guidance was mixed with various other sources.

There is another basic cause that has operated in creating this difference. They of the first generation did not approach the Qur'an for the
purpose of acquiring culture and information. None of them came to the
Qur'an to increase his sum total of knowledge or to solve some scientific
or legal problem. He rather turned to the Qur'an to find out what the
Almighty had prescribed for him and for his life.

He did not read many verses of the Qur'an in one session, as he understood that this would lay an unbearable burden of duties and responsibilities on his shoulders. At most he would read ten verses, memorize them,
and then act upon them. This understanding opened the doors to spiritual
fulfillment and to knowledge. Action became easy, the weight of responsibilities became light, and the Qur'an became a part of their personalities, mingling with their lives and characters so that they became living
examples of faith—a faith not hidden in intellects or books but expressing
itself in a dynamic movement that changed the course of life.

We must return to that pure source from which those people derived
their guidance, the source that is free from any mixing or pollution. We
must return to it to derive from it our concepts of the nature of the universe, the nature of human existence, and the relationship of these two
with God. From it we must also derive our concepts of life, our principles
of government, politics, economics, and all other aspects of life. We must
return to it with a sense of instruction for obedience and action, and not
for academic discussion and enjoyment.

Our primary purpose is to know what way of life is demanded of us by
the Qur'an, the total view of the universe that the Qur'an wants us to have,
what is the nature of our knowledge of God taught to us by the Qur'an, the
kind of morals and manners that are enjoined by it, and the kind of legal
and constitutional system it asks us to establish in the world.

Our aim is first to change ourselves so that we may later change the
society. Our foremost objective is to change the practices of this society at
its very roots—this system that is fundamentally at variance with Islam
and that, with the help of force and oppression, is keeping us from living
the sort of life that is demanded by our Creator.

The Characteristics of the Islamic Society and the Correct Method for Its Formation

Throughout every period of human history the call toward God has had one nature. Its purpose is "Islam," which means to bring human beings into submission to God, to free them from servitude to other human beings so that they may devote themselves to God, to deliver them from the clutches of human lordship and manmade laws, value systems, and traditions so that they will acknowledge the sovereignty and authority of God and follow his law in all spheres of life.

The Islam of Muhammad came for this purpose, as well as the messages of the earlier prophets. The entire universe is under the authority of God, and man, being a small part of it, necessarily obeys the physical laws governing the universe. It is also necessary that the same authority be acknowledged as the law giver for human life.

Man should not cut himself off from this authority to develop a separate system and a separate scheme of life. The growth of a human being, his conditions of health and disease, and his life and death are under the scheme of those natural laws that come from God; even in the consequences of his voluntary actions he is helpless before the universal laws. Man cannot change the practice of God in the laws prevailing in the universe. It is therefore desirable that he should also follow Islam in those aspects of his life in which he is given a choice and should make the Divine Law the arbiter in all matters of life so that there may be harmony between man and the rest of the universe.

Jahiliyyah [ignorance of divine guidance], on the other hand, is one man's lordship over another, and in this respect it is against the system of the universe and brings the involuntary aspect of human life into conflict with its voluntary aspect. This was that *jahiliyyah* that confronted every prophet of God, including the last Prophet, in their call toward submission to one God. This *jahiliyyah* is not an abstract theory; in fact, under certain circumstances it has no theory at all. It always takes the form of a living movement in a society that has its own leadership, its own concepts and values, and its own traditions, habits, and feelings. It is an organized society, and there is close cooperation and loyalty between its individuals. It crushes all elements that seem to be dangerous to its personality.

Jahiliyyah controls the practical world, and for its support there is a living and active organization. In this situation, mere theoretical efforts to fight it cannot even be equal, much less superior, to it. When the purpose is to abolish the existing system and to replace it with a new system, then it stands to reason that this new system should also come into the battlefield as an organized movement and a viable group.

It should come into the battlefield with a determination that its strategy, its social organization, and the relationship between its individuals should be firmer and more powerful than the existing *jahili* [pre-Islam] system. The theoretical foundation of Islam, in every period of history, has been to witness "La ilaha illa Allah"—"There is no deity except God"—which means to bear witness that the only true deity is God. Without this complete acceptance of "La ilaha illa Allah," which differentiates the one who says he is a Muslim from a non-Muslim, there cannot be any practical significance to this utterance, nor will it have any weight according to Islamic law.

Theoretically, to establish it means that people should devote their entire lives in submission to God, should not decide any affair on their own, but must refer to God's injunctions concerning it and follow them. We know of God's guidance through only one source, that is, through the messenger of God—peace be on him. Thus in the second part of the Islamic creed, we bear witness, "Wa ashhadu anna Muhammadar Rasul Allah"—"And I bear witness that Muhammad is the messenger of God." It is therefore necessary that Islam's theoretical foundation—belief—materialize in the form of an organized and active group from the very beginning. It is necessary that this group separate itself from the *jahili* society, becoming independent and distinct from the active and organized *jahili* society whose aim is to block Islam.

The center of this new group should be a new leadership. A person who bears witness that there is no deity except God and that Muhammad is God's messenger should cut off his relationship of loyalty from the *jahili* society, which he has forsaken, and from *jahili* leadership, whether it be in the guise of priests, magicians, or astrologers, or in the form of political, social, or economic leadership. He will have to give his complete loyalty to the new Islamic movement and to the Muslim leadership.

There is no other way for the revival of Islam in the shade of *jahiliyyah*, in whatever age or country it appears, except to follow its natural character and to develop it into a movement.

Jihad in the Cause of God

The great scholar Ibn Qayyim has written *The Prophet's Treatment of the Unbelievers and the Hypocrites from the Beginning of His Messengership Until His Death*. In this work this scholar sums up the nature of Islamic jihad:

> God commanded the Prophet to warn his near relatives, then his people, then the Arabs who were around them, then all of Arabia, and finally the whole world. Thus for thirteen years after the beginning of his Messengership, he called people to God through preaching, without fighting or *jizyah*, and was commanded to restrain himself and to practice patience and forbearance.
>
> Then he was commanded to migrate, and later permission was given to fight. Then he was commanded to fight those who fought him, and to restrain himself from those who did not make war with him.
>
> Later he was commanded to fight the polytheists until God's religion was fully established. After the command for jihad came, the nonbelievers were divided into three categories: one, those with whom there was peace; two, the people with whom the Muslims were at war; and three, the *dhimmies*.
>
> It was commanded that as long as the nonbelievers with whom he had a peace treaty met their obligations, he should fulfill the articles of the treaty, but if they broke this treaty, then they should be given notice of having broken it; until then, no war should be declared. If they persisted, then he should fight with them.
>
> It was also explained that war should be declared against those from among the People of the Book who declare open enmity, until they agree to pay *jizyah*, or accept Islam.
>
> Concerning the polytheists and the hypocrites, it was commanded that jihad be declared against them and that they be treated harshly.
>
> The people with treaties eventually became Muslims, so there were only two kinds left: people at war and *dhimmies*. The people at war were always afraid of him. Now the people of the whole world were of three kinds: one, the Muslims who believed in him; two, those with whom he had peace and the opponents who kept fighting him. As far as the hypocrites were concerned, God commanded the Prophet to accept their appearances and leave their intentions to God and carry on jihad against them by argument and persuasion.

In this description we find a summary of the stages of Islamic jihad presented in an excellent manner. In this summary we find all the distinctive and far-reaching characteristics of the dynamic movement of the true religion; we should ponder over them for deep study. Here, however, we will confine ourselves to a few explanatory remarks.

First, the method of this religion is very practical. This movement treats people as they actually are and uses resources in accordance with practical conditions. This movement uses the methods of preaching and persuasion for reforming ideas and beliefs and it uses physical power and jihad for abolishing the organizations and authorities of the *jahili* system, which prevent people from reforming their ideas and beliefs. This movement does not confine itself to mere preaching to confront physical power, as it also does not use compulsion for changing the ideas of people. These two principles are equally important in the method of this religion. Its purpose is to free those people who wish to be freed from enslavement to men so that they may serve God alone.

The second aspect of this religion is that it is a practical movement that progresses stage by stage, and at every stage it provides resources according to the practical needs of the situation and prepares the ground for the next one. It does not face practical problems with abstract theories, nor does it confront various stages with unchangeable means. Those who talk about jihad in Islam and quote Qur'anic verses do not take into account this aspect, nor do they understand the nature of the various stages through which this movement develops, or the relationship of the verses revealed at various occasions with each stage. Thus, when they speak about jihad, they speak clumsily and mix up the various stages, distorting the whole concept of jihad.

This is because they regard every verse of the Qur'an as if it were the final principle of this religion. This group of thinkers, who are a product of the sorry state of the present Muslim generation, have nothing but the label of Islam and have laid down their spiritual and rational arms in defeat. They say, "Islam has prescribed only defensive war!"

When writers with defeatist and apologetic mentalities write about "jihad in Islam," trying to remove this "blot" from Islam, then they are mixing up two things: first, that this religion forbids the imposition of its belief by force, while on the other hand it tries to annihilate all those political and material powers that stand between people and Islam. These two principles have no relation to one another, nor is there room to mix them. In spite of this, these defeatist-type people try to mix the two aspects and want to confine jihad to what today is called "defensive war."

The Islamic jihad has no relationship to modern warfare, either in its causes or in the way in which it is conducted. The causes of Islamic jihad should be sought in the very nature of Islam and its role in the world, in its high principles, which have been given to it by God.

It means a challenge to all kinds and forms of systems that are based on the concept of the sovereignty of man; in other words, where man has usurped the divine attribute. Any system in which the final decisions are referred to human beings, and in which the sources of all authority are human, defiles human beings by designating others than God as lords over men. This declaration means that the usurped authority of God be returned to him and the usurpers be thrown out—those who by themselves devise laws for others to follow, thus elevating themselves to the status of lords and reducing others to the status of slaves.

To establish God's rule means that his laws be enforced and that the final decision in all affairs be according to these laws. The establishment of the dominion of God on earth and abolishing of the dominion of man cannot be achieved only through preaching. Those who have usurped the authority of God and are oppressing God's creatures are not going to give up their power merely through preaching; if it had been so, the task of establishing God's religion in the world would have been very easy for the prophets of God!

If through "preaching" beliefs and ideas are confronted, through "the movement" material obstacles are tackled. Foremost among these is that political power that rests on a complex yet interrelated ideological, racial, class, social, and economic support. Thus these two—preaching and the movement—united, confront "the human situation" with all the necessary methods. For the achievement of the freedom of man on earth it is necessary that these two methods should work side by side. This is a very important point and cannot be overemphasized.

If the actual life of human beings is found to be different from Islam's declaration of freedom, then it becomes incumbent upon Islam to enter the field with preaching as well as the movement, and to strike hard at all those political powers that force people to bow before them and that rule over them, unmindful of the commandments of God.

After annihilating the tyrannical force, whether it be in a political or a racial form, or in the form of class distinctions within the same race, Islam establishes a new social, economic, and political system in which the concept of the freedom of man is applied in practice.

It is not the intention of Islam to force its beliefs on people, but Islam is not merely "belief." As we have pointed out, Islam is a declaration of the freedom of man from servitude to other men. Thus it strives from the beginning to abolish all those systems and governments that are based on the rule of man over men and the servitude of one human being to another. When Islam releases people from this political pressure and presents to them its spiritual message, appealing to their reason, it gives them complete freedom to accept or not to accept its beliefs.

However, this freedom does not mean that they can make their desires their gods, or that they can choose to remain in the servitude of other human beings, making some men lords over others. Whatever system is to be established in the world ought to be on the authority of God. Then every individual is free, under the protection of this universal system, to adopt any belief he wishes to adopt. This is the only way in which "the religion" can be purified for God alone. The word "religion" includes more than belief; "religion" actually means a way of life, and in Islam this is based on belief. But in an Islamic system there is room for all kinds of people to follow their own beliefs, while obeying the laws of the country that are themselves based on the divine authority.

Anyone who understands this particular character of this religion will also understand the place of *jihad bis saif* [striving through fighting], which is to clear the way for striving through preaching in the application of the Islamic movement. He will understand that Islam is not a "defensive movement" in the narrow sense that today is technically called a "defensive war." This narrow meaning is ascribed to it by those who are under the pressure of circumstances and are defeated by the wily attacks of the orientalists, who distort the concept of Islamic jihad.

If we insist on calling Islamic jihad a defensive movement, then we must change the meaning of the word "defense" and mean by it "the defense of man" against all those elements that limit his freedom. These elements take the form of beliefs and concepts, as well as of political systems, based on economic, racial, or class distinctions. When Islam first came into existence, the world was full of such systems, and the present-day *jahiliyyah* also has various kinds of such systems.

When we take this broad meaning of the word "defense," we understand the true character of Islam, and that it is a universal proclamation of the freedom of man from servitude to other men, the establishment of the sovereignty of God and his lordship throughout the world, and the implementation of the rule of the divine sharia in human affairs.

As to persons who attempt to defend the concept of Islamic jihad by interpreting it in the narrow sense of the current concept of defensive war, and who do research to prove that the battles fought in Islamic jihad were all for the defense of the homeland of Islam—some of them considering the homeland of Islam to be just the Arabian peninsula—against the aggression of neighboring powers, they lack understanding of the nature of Islam and its primary aim. Such an attempt is nothing but a product of a mind defeated by the present difficult conditions and by the attacks of the treacherous orientalists on the Islamic jihad.

Since the objective of the message of Islam is a decisive declaration of man's freedom, not merely on the philosophical plane but also in the actual conditions of life, it must employ jihad. It is immaterial whether the homeland of Islam—in the true Islamic sense, Dar al-Islam—is in a condition of peace or whether it is threatened by its neighbors. When Islam strives for peace, its objective is not that superficial peace that requires that only that part of the earth where the followers of Islam are residing remain secure. The peace that Islam desires is that the religion has the obedience of all the world's people.

The command to refrain from fighting during the Meccan period was a temporary stage in a long journey. The same reason was operative during the early days of *hijra* [the withdrawal of Muhammad and his followers to Medina in 622] but after these early stages, the reason for jihad was not merely to defend Medina. Indeed, its defense was necessary, but this was not the ultimate aim. The aim was to protect the resources and the center of the movement—the movement for freeing mankind and demolishing the obstacles that prevented mankind from attaining this freedom.

Those who look for causes of a defensive nature in the history of the expansion of Islam are caught by the aggressive attacks of the orientalists at a time when Muslims possess neither glory nor do they possess Islam. However, by God's grace, there are those who are standing firm on the issue that Islam is a universal declaration of the freedom of man on the earth from every authority except God's authority, and that the religion ought to be purified for God; and they keep writing concerning the Islamic jihad.

But the Islamic movement does not need any arguments taken from the literature, as it stands on the clear verses of the Qur'an:

> They ought to fight in the way of God who have sold the life of this world for the life of the Hereafter; and whoever fights in the way of God and is killed or becomes victorious, to him shall We give a great reward.

Fight against those among the People of the Book who do not believe in God and the Last Day, who do not forbid what God and his Messenger have forbidden, and who do not consider the true religion as their way of life, until they are subdued and pay *Jizyah*.

The Jews say: "Ezra is the Son of God," and the Christians say: "The Messiah is the Son of God." These are mere sayings from their mouths, following those who preceded them and disbelieved. God will assail them; how they are perverted!

They have taken their rabbis and priests as lords other that God, and the Messiah, son of Mary; and they were commanded to worship none but One God. There is no deity but he, glory be to him above what they associate with him! They desire to extinguish God's light with their mouths, and God intends to perfect his light, although the unbelievers may be in opposition.

The reason for jihad exists in the nature of Islam's message and in the actual conditions it finds in human societies, and not merely in the necessity for defense, which may be temporary and of limited extent. A Muslim fights with his wealth and his person "in the way of God" for the sake of these values in which neither personal gain nor greed is a motive for him.

Those who say that Islamic jihad was merely for the defense of the "homeland of Islam" diminish the greatness of the Islamic way of life and consider it less important than their "homeland." This is not the Islamic point of view, and their view is a creation of the modern age and is completely alien to Islamic consciousness. Defense is not the ultimate objective of the Islamic jihad but is a means of establishing the divine authority within it so that it becomes the headquarters for the movement of Islam, which is then to be carried throughout the earth to the whole of mankind.

As we have described earlier, there are many practical obstacles in establishing God's rule on earth, such as the power of the state, the social system, and traditions and, in general, the whole human environment. Islam uses force only to remove these obstacles so that there may not remain any wall between Islam and individual human beings.

It may happen that the enemies of Islam may consider it expedient not to take any action against Islam, if Islam leaves them alone in their geographical boundaries to continue the lordship of some men over others and does not extend its message and its declaration of universal freedom within their domain. But Islam cannot agree to this unless they submit to its authority by paying *jizyah*, which will be a guarantee that they have opened their doors for the preaching of Islam and will not put any obstacle in its way through the power of the state.

Indeed, Islam has the right to take the initiative. Islam is not a heritage of any particular race or country; this is God's religion and it is for the whole world. It has the right to destroy all obstacles in the form of institutions and traditions that limit man's freedom of choice. It does not attack individuals, nor does it force them to accept its beliefs; it attacks institutions and traditions to release human beings from their poisonous influences, which distort human nature and curtail human freedom.

Thus wherever an Islamic community exists it has a God-given right to step forward and take control of the political authority so that it may establish the divine system on earth. When God restrained Muslims from jihad for a certain period, it was a question of strategy rather than of principle.

It is clear that a Muslim community cannot be formed or continue to exist until it attains sufficient power to confront the existing *jahili* society. This power must be at all levels; that is to say, the power of belief and concept, the power of training and moral character, the power to organize and sustain a community, and such physical power as is necessary, if not to dominate, at least to hold itself against the onslaught of the *jahili* society.

But what is the *jahili* society, and by what method does Islam confront it? The *jahili* society is any society other than the Muslim society; and if we want a more specific definition, we may say that any society is a *jahili* society that does not dedicate itself to submission to God alone, in its beliefs and ideas in its observances of worship, and in its legal regulations. According to this definition, all the societies existing in the world today are *jahili*.

All Jewish and Christian societies are *jahili* societies. They have distorted the original beliefs and ascribe certain attributes of God to other beings. This association with God has taken many forms, such as the worship of God or the Trinity; sometimes it is expressed in a concept of God that is remote from the true reality of God.

These societies are *jahili* also because their forms of worship and their customs and manners are derived from their false and distorted beliefs. They are also *jahili* societies because their institutions and their laws are not based on submission to God alone. They neither accept the rule of God nor do they consider God's commandments as the only valid basis of all laws; on the contrary, they have established assemblies of men that have absolute power to legislate laws, thus usurping the right that belongs to God alone.

The Universal Law

Islam constructs its foundation of belief and action on the principle of total submission to God alone. Its beliefs, forms of worship, and rules of life are uniformly an expression of this submission and are a practical interpretation of the declaration that there is no deity except God. The details of life are derived from the practice of the Prophet and are a practical consequence of the declaration that Muhammad is the messenger of God.

Islam builds its entire structure in such a way that these two parts of the declaration determine its system and its characteristics. When Islam builds its structure in this manner, giving it a separate and unique position among all other systems known to man, then Islam actually becomes harmonious with the universal law, which is operative not only in human existence but throughout the whole universe as well. According to the Islamic concept, the whole universe has been created by God. The universe came into existence when God willed it, and then he ordained certain natural laws that it follows and according to which all its various parts operate harmoniously:

> All unconditionally submit to the Will of God and to the laws of his creation. He who has created the universe and man, has also prescribed a sharia for his voluntary actions. If man follows this law, then his life is in harmony with his own nature. From this point of view, this sharia is also a part of that universal law which governs the entire universe, including the physical and biological aspects of man.

This obedience to sharia is necessary for the sake of this harmony, even more necessary than the establishment of the Islamic belief, as no individual can be truly Muslim until he wholly submits to God alone in the manner taught by the Prophet. Total harmony between human life and the law of the universe is entirely beneficial for mankind, as this is the only guarantee against any kind of discord in life. Only in this state will they be at peace with themselves and at peace with the universe, living in accord with its laws and its movements. In the same way, they will have peace of mind, as their actions will agree with their true natural demands, with no conflict between the two. Indeed, the sharia of God harmonizes the external behavior of man with his internal nature in an easy way. When a man makes peace with his own nature, peace and cooperation among individuals follow automatically, as they all live together under one system, which is a part of the general system of the universe.

Islam Is the Real Civilization

Islam knows only two kinds of societies, the Islamic and the *jahili*. The Islamic society is that which follows Islam in belief and ways of worship, in law and organization, in morals and manners. The *jahili* society is that which does not follow Islam and in which neither Islamic belief and concepts, nor Islamic values or standards, or Islamic laws and regulations are cared for. *Jahili* society appears in various forms, all of them ignorant of the divine guidance. Neither the sharia nor the values prescribed by God find any place in this scheme of life. In this society, people are permitted to go to mosques, churches, and synagogues; yet it does not tolerate people's demanding that the sharia be applied in their daily affairs. Thus, such a society denies or suspends God's sovereignty on earth. Because of this behavior, such a society does not follow the religion of God as defined by him.

The Islamic society is, by its very nature, the only civilized society, and the *jahili* societies, in all their various forms, are backward societies. It is necessary to elucidate this great truth. The Western concept of civilization was at one time my standard and this once prevented me from seeing with clear and penetrating vision. However, later I saw very clearly that the Muslim society was the civilized society.

It is necessary that we clarify the point that legislation is not limited only to legal matters, as some people assign this narrow meaning to the sharia. The fact is that attitudes, the way of living, the values, criteria, habits, and traditions are all legislated and affect people. Only Islamic society is unique in that the authority belongs to God alone; and man, cutting off his chains of servitude to other human beings, enters into the service of God and thus attains that real and complete freedom that is the focus of human civilization. Only Islam has the distinction of basing the fundamental binding relationship in its society on belief; and on the basis of this belief, black and white and red and yellow, Arabs and Greeks, Persians and Africans, and all nations that inhabit the earth become one community.

If the family is the basis of the society, and the basis of the family is the division of labor between husband and wife, and the upbringing of children is the most important function of the family, then such a society is indeed civilized. In the Islamic system of life, this kind of a family provides the environment under which human values and morals develop and grow in the new generation; these values and morals cannot exist apart from the family unit. If, on the other hand, free sexual relationships and illegitimate children become the basis of a society, and if the relationship between man and woman is based on lust, passion, and impulse and the division of work is not based on family responsibility and natural gifts; if woman's role is merely to be attractive, sexy, and flirtatious, and if woman is freed from her basic responsibility of bringing up children; and if, on her own or under social demand, she prefers to become a hostess or a stewardess in a hotel or ship or air company, thus spending her ability for material productivity rather than in the training of human beings, because material production is considered to be more important, more valuable, and more honorable than the development of human character, then such a civilization is "backward" from the human point of view, or *jahili* in the Islamic terminology.

The family system and the relationship between the sexes determine the whole character of a society and whether it is backward or civilized, *jahili* or Islamic. Those societies that give ascendance to physical desires and animalistic morals cannot be considered civilized, no matter how much progress they may make in industry or science. In these societies, illegitimate sexual relationships, even homosexuality, are not considered immoral. The meaning of ethics is limited to economic affairs or sometimes to political affairs, which fall into the category of "government interests." Among *jahili* societies, writers, journalists, and editors advise both married and unmarried people that free sexual relationships are not immoral. However, it is immoral if a boy uses his partner, or a girl uses her partner, for sex while feeling no love in his or her heart. It is bad if a wife continues to guard her chastity while her love for her husband has vanished; it is admirable if she finds another lover.

The Islamic Concept and Culture

A Muslim cannot go to any source other than God for guidance in matters of faith, in the concept of life, acts of worship, morals, values and standards, principles of economics and political affairs, and interpretation of historical processes. It is, therefore, his duty that he should learn all these from a Muslim whose piety and character are beyond reproach. However, a Muslim can go to a Muslim or to a non-Muslim to learn abstract sciences such as chemistry, physics, biology, astronomy, medicine, industry, agriculture, administration (limited to its technical aspects), technology, military arts, and similar sciences and arts; although the fundamental principle is that when the Muslim community comes into existence it should provide experts in all these fields in abundance.

If a proper atmosphere is not provided under which these sciences and arts develop in a Muslim society, the whole society will be considered sinful; but as long as these conditions are not attained, it is permitted for a Muslim to learn them from a Muslim or a non-Muslim and to gain experience under his direction, without any distinction of religion. As for the explanation of the origin of the universe and the origin of the life of man, they are part of metaphysics and thus their position is similar to legal matters, rules, and regulations that order human life. These indirectly affect man's beliefs; it is therefore not permissible for a Muslim to learn them from anyone other than a God-fearing and pious Muslim.

For example, Darwinist biology goes beyond the scope of its observations, without any rhyme or reason and only for the sake of expressing an opinion, in making the assumption that to explain the beginning of life and its evolution there is no need to assume a power outside the physical world. Concerning these matters, the true guidance from his Sustainer is sufficient for a Muslim. This guidance toward belief and complete submission to God alone is so superior to all man's speculative attempts in these affairs that they appear utterly ridiculous and absurd.

The statement that "Culture is the human heritage" and that it has no country, nationality, or religion is correct only in relation to science and technology—as long as we do not jump the boundary of these sciences and delve into metaphysical interpretations and start explaining the purpose of man and his historical role in philosophical terms. Beyond this limited meaning, this statement about culture is one of the tricks played by world Jewry, whose purpose is to eliminate all limitations, especially the limitations imposed by faith and religion, so that the Jews may penetrate into body politic of the whole world and then may be free to perpetuate their evil designs.

At the top of the list of these activities is usury, the aim of which is that all the wealth of mankind end up in the hands of Jewish financial institutions that run on interest.

One ought to remember the fact that the experimental method, which is the dynamic spirit of modern Europe's industrial culture, did not originate in Europe but originated in the Islamic universities of Andalusia and of the East. The principle of the experimental method was an offshoot of the Islamic concept and its explanations of the physical world, its phenomena, its forces, and its secrets. Later, by adopting the experimental method, Europe entered into the period of scientific revival, which led it step by step to great scientific heights. Meanwhile, the Muslim world gradually drifted away from Islam, as a consequence of which the scientific movement first became inert and later ended completely.

We must be watchful in who we learn from. It would be extremely shortsighted of us to fall into the illusion that when the Jews and Christians discuss Islamic beliefs or Islamic history, or when they make proposals concerning Muslim society or Muslim politics or economics, they will be doing it with good intentions or with the welfare of the Muslims at heart.

We must also keep in mind that the entire scientific movement in Europe started with Godlessness and this changed the entire character of European thought. The effect of this hostility of the scientific community toward the church did not remain limited to the church or to its beliefs but was directed against all religion, so much so that all sciences turned against religion, whether they were speculative philosophy or technical or abstract sciences having nothing to do with religion. The Western ways of thought and all the sciences started on the foundation of these poisonous influences with an enmity toward all religion, and in particular with greater hostility toward Islam.

This enmity toward Islam is especially pronounced and many times is the result of a well-thought-out scheme, the object of which is first to shake the foundations of Islamic beliefs and then gradually to demolish the structure of Muslim society. If, in spite of knowing this, we rely on Western ways of thought, even in teaching the Islamic sciences, it will be an unforgivable blindness on our part. Indeed, it becomes incumbent on us, while learning purely scientific or technological subjects for which we have no other sources except Western sources, to remain on guard and keep these sciences away from philosophical speculations, as these philosophical speculations are against Islam. A slight influence from them can pollute the clear spring of Islam.

A Muslim's Nationality and His Belief

This Islamic homeland is a refuge for any who accepts the Islamic sharia to be the law of the state. But any place where the Islamic sharia is not enforced and where Islam is not dominant becomes the home of Hostility (Dar al-Harb). A Muslim will remain prepared to fight against it, whether it be his birthplace or a place where his relatives reside or where his property or any other material interests are located. And thus Muhammad— peace be on him—fought against the city of Mecca, although it was his birthplace, and his relatives lived there, and he and his companions had houses and property there that they had left when they migrated; yet the soil of Mecca did not become Dar al-Islam for him and his followers until it surrendered to Islam and the sharia became operative in it.

Only this is Islam, not the soil, not the race, not the lineage, not the tribe, and not the family. Islam freed all humanity from the chains of blood relationships—the biological chains—so that they might rise above the angels. The homeland of the Muslim, in which he lives and which he defends, is not a piece of land. The nationality of the Muslim, by which he is identified, is not the nationality determined by a government. The flag of the Muslim, which he honors and under which he is martyred, is not the flag of a country. The victory of the Muslim is not a military victory.

The victory is achieved under the banner of faith, and under no other banners; the striving is purely for the sake of God, for the success of his religion and his law, for the protection of Dar al-Islam, the particulars of which we have described above, and for no other purpose. It is not for the spoils or for fame, nor for the honor of a country or nation, nor for the mere protection of one's family except when supporting them against religious persecution. The honor of martyrdom is achieved only when one is fighting in the cause of God, and if one is killed for any other purpose this honor will not be attained.

The callers to Islam should not have any superficial doubts in their hearts concerning the nature of *jahiliyyah* and the nature of Islam. Through these doubts many are led to confusion. Indeed, there is no Islam in a land where Islam is not dominant and where its sharia is not established; and that place is not Dar al-Islam where Islam's way of life and its laws are not practiced. There is nothing beyond faith except unbelief, nothing beyond Islam except *jahiliyyah*, nothing beyond the truth except falsehood.

Far-Reaching Changes

It is not the function of Islam to compromise with the concepts of *jahiliyyah* that are current in the world or to coexist in the same land together with a *jahili* system. This was not the case when it first appeared in the world, nor will it be today or in the future. Islam cannot accept any mixing with *jahiliyyah*, either in its concept or in the modes of living. Either Islam will remain, or *jahiliyyah*: Islam cannot accept or agree to a situation that is half-Islam and half-*jahiliyyah*. In this respect Islam's stand is very clear. It says that the truth is one and cannot be divided; if it is not the truth, then it must be falsehood. The mixing and coexistence of the truth and falsehood is impossible.

The foremost duty of Islam in this world is to depose *jahiliyyah* from the leadership of man, and to take the leadership into its own hands and enforce the particular way of life that is its permanent feature. The purpose of this rightly guided leadership is the good and success of mankind. The intention is to raise human beings to that high position that God has chosen for them and to free them from the slavery of desires. Islam does not sanction the rule of selfish desires. It has come to abolish all such concepts, laws, customs, and traditions, and to replace them with a new concept of human life, to create a new world on the foundation of submission to the Creator.

Jahiliyyah is evil and corrupt, whether it be of the ancient or modern variety. Its outward manifestations may be different during different epochs. When we call people to Islam, it is our duty to make them understand that it is not one of the manmade religions or ideologies, nor is it a manmade system—with various names, banners, and paraphernalia—but it is Islam, and nothing else. Islam has its own permanent personality and permanent concept and permanent modes. Islam guarantees for mankind a blessing greater than all these manmade systems.

We need not rationalize Islam to the West, need not appease their desires and distorted concepts. We will be extremely outspoken with them: The ignorance in which you are living makes you impure, and God wants to purify you; the customs that you follow are defiling, and God wants to cleanse you; the life you are living is low, and God wants to uplift you; the condition that you are in is troublesome, depressing, and base and God wants to give you ease, mercy, and goodness. Islam will change your concepts, your modes of living, and your values.

Islam does not take its justifications from the *jahili* system and its evil derivatives. And these "civilizations," which have dazzled many and have defeated their spirits, are nothing but a *jahili* system at heart, and this system is erroneous, hollow, and worthless in comparison with Islam. The argument that the people living under it are in a better condition than the people of a so-called Islamic country or "the Islamic world" has no weight. The people in these countries have reached this wretched state by abandoning Islam, and not because they are Muslims. The argument that Islam presents to people is this: Most certainly Islam is better beyond imagination. It has come to change *jahiliyyah*, not to continue it; to elevate mankind from its depravity, and not to bless its manifestations that have taken the garb of "civilization."

We ought not to be defeated to such an extent that we start looking for similarities with Islam in the current systems or in some current religions or in some current ideas; we reject these systems in the East as well as in the West. We reject them all, as indeed they are retrogressive and in opposition to the direction toward which Islam intends to take mankind. When we address people in this fashion and present to them the basic message of the comprehensive concept of Islam, the justification for changing from one concept to another, from one mode of living to another, will come from the very depths of their being. But we will not address them with this ineffective argument, saying: "Come from a system which is currently established to a system not yet applied; it will make only a little change in the established order. You should have no objection; you can continue to do what you have been doing. It will not bother you except to ask for a few changes in your habits, manners, and inclinations, and will preserve for you whatever pleases you and will not touch it except very slightly."

On the surface this method seems easy, but there is no attraction in it; moreover, it is not based on the truth. The truth is that Islam not only changes concepts and attitudes, but also the system and modes, laws and customs, since this change is so fundamental that no relationship can remain with the *jahili* way of life, the life that mankind is living.

There is nothing in our Islam of which we are ashamed or anxious about defending; there is nothing in it to be smuggled to the people with deception, nor do we muffle the loud truth that it proclaims. This is the defeated mentality, defeated before the West and before the East and before this and that mode of *jahiliyyah*, which is found in some Muslims who search for resemblances to Islam in manmade systems. A person who feels the need of defense, justification, and apology is not capable of presenting Islam to people. Indeed, he is a person who lives the life of *jahiliyyah*, hollow and full of contradictions, defects, and evils. They confuse Islam's true nature by their defense, as if Islam were something accused standing at trial, anxious for its own defense.

Our first task is to replace this *jahiliyyah* with Islamic ideas and traditions. This cannot be brought about by agreeing with jahiliyyah and going along a few steps with it from the very beginning, as some of us think we ought to do, for this will simply mean that from the very beginning we have accepted defeat.

This Is the Road

The struggle between the Believers and their enemies is in essence a struggle of belief, and not in any way of anything else. The enemies are angered only because of their faith, enraged only because of their belief. This is not a political or an economic or a racial struggle; had it been any of these, its settlement would have been easy. But essentially it was a struggle between beliefs—either unbelief or faith, either *jahiliyyah* or Islam.

The enemies of the believers may wish to change this struggle into an economic or political or racial struggle, so that the believers become confused concerning the true nature of the struggle and the flame of belief in their hearts becomes extinguished. The believers must not be deceived and must understand that this is a trick. The enemy, by changing the nature of the struggle, intends to deprive them of their weapon of true victory, the victory that can take any form, be it the victory of the freedom, or dominance in the world—as a consequence of the freedom of spirit—as happened in the case of the first generation of Muslims.

We see an example of this today in the attempts of Christendom to try to deceive us by distorting history and saying that the Crusades were a form of imperialism. The truth of the matter is that the latter-day imperialism is but a mask for the crusading spirit, since it is not possible for it to appear in its true form, as it was possible in the Middle Ages. The unveiled crusading spirit was smashed against the rock of the faith of Muslim leadership, which came from various elements, including Saladin the Kurd and Turan Shah, who forgot the differences of nationalities and remembered their belief, and were victorious under the banner of Islam.

CHAPTER 4
The Neglected Obligation

MUHAMMAD AL-SALAM FARAJ

Muhammad al-Salaam Faraj was an Egyptian engineer who was one of Egypt's most important Islamic revolutionary theorists and organizers. Faraj was part of the post-1966 salafist movement and was inspired by Sayyid Qutb and his interpretations of the Islamic struggle. He rejected many of his contemporary salafis, including the Muslim Brotherhood, for seeking integration into the political process.

Splitting away from a group called Jama'at al-Jihad (Group of Holy Struggle), Faraj formed his own group of the same name in 1981. This group rapidly expanded, absorbing other cells (including former Takfir w'al Hijra cells), and began carrying out terrorist attacks against the state. The culmination of this terror campaign was the assassination of Egypt's President Anwar Sadat at an army parade. The assassin was an army officer, Lt. Khalid Islambouli, who was able to get close to the president because he was part of the parade. This attack, which was personally sanctioned by Faraj, demonstrated the effectiveness of his policy of infiltration of the regime.

However, because al-Jihad had not put significant time and effort into setting up a clandestine underground network, its members were easily rounded up by the security forces. Al-Jihad's campaign began and ended in 1981, and Faraj himself was executed in April 1982. His "Neglected Obligation" provides the ideological rationale many jihadist groups have used to justify violent means to overthrow local governments.

Islam Approaches

T he establishment of an Islamic state and the reintroduction of the caliphate were predicted by Muhammad. Moreover, it is the command of the Lord for which every Muslim should exert every conceivable effort in order to execute it.

Muhammad said, "God showed me all corners of the earth. I saw its East and its West, and that my Community will possess of it what he showed me from it." This has not until now come about, since there are countries that the Muslims have not conquered; however, it shall come about.

The Establishment of an Islamic State

This is a duty that is rejected by some Muslims and neglected by others, although the proof of the obligation to establish a state is clear and made obvious by the Book of God; "and that you must rule between them according to what God sent do God's prescripts are an obligation for the Muslims." Hence the establishment of an Islamic state is obligatory. If that state cannot be established without war, then that becomes an obligation also. So it is obligatory for every Muslim to seriously strive for the return of the caliphate.

The House in Which We Live

Here a question appears: Do we live in an Islamic state? One of the characteristics of such a state is that it is ruled by the laws of Islam. Imam Abu Hanifah gave as his opinion that the House of Islam changes into the House of Unbelief if three conditions are fulfilled: 1) if it is ruled by other laws than those of Islam, 2) the disappearance of safety for the Muslim inhabitants, 3) its being adjacent or close . . . and this means that the House of Islam is close to the House of Unbelief to such an extent that this is a source of danger to the Muslims. The state (of Egypt in which we live today) is ruled by the laws of Unbelief although the majority of its inhabitants are Muslims.

The Ruler Who Rules by Laws Other Than Those That God Sent Down

The laws by which the Muslims are ruled today are the laws of Unbelief, they are actually codes of law that were made by infidels who subjected the Muslims to these laws. After the disappearance of the caliphate in 1924, the laws of Islam were removed in their entirety.

Ibn Kathir says: "God disapproves of whosoever rebels against God's laws, which are clear and precise and that contain everything which is good and that forbid everything that is bad. Whosoever does so is an infidel and he must be fought until he returns to the rule of God and his Apostle, and until he rules by no other law than God's law."

The rulers of this age have rebelled against the religion of Islam in multiple ways to such a degree that there is little doubt as to how to judge people who follow the ways of these rulers.

The Rulers of the Muslims Today Are in Apostasy from Islam

The rulers of this age are in apostasy from Islam. They were raised at the tables of imperialism, be it Crusaderism, or communism, or Zionism. They carry nothing from Islam but their names, even though they pray and fast and claim to be Muslim. It is a well-established rule of Islamic law that the punishment of an apostate will be heavier than the punishment of someone who is by origin an infidel (and has never been a Muslim). For instance, an apostate is to be killed even if he is unable to carry arms or go to war. It is the view of the majority of jurists that an apostate has to be killed, and this is in accordance with the opinions held in all of the Islamic schools of law.

The leading scholars of Islam agree that a group of people who refuse to carry out part of the clear and reliably transmitted duties of Islam have to be fought when they publicly confess to be Muslim by pronouncing the Islamic confession of faith (There is no god but God and Muhammad is his Apostle) but at the same time refuse to carry out the prayer ceremonies and to pay the *zakat* tax, or to keep the fast of the month of Ramadan.

Ibn Taymiyah's Fatwas against the Mongols Apply Today

Because of the similarity of today's Crusaders to the Mongols we think it
proper to quote some of Ibn Taymiyah's [a religious scholar at the time of
the Mongol invasions] fatwas on how to judge these people.

How to Judge Helping and Supporting Them?

Ibn Taymiyah says, "To help those who rebel against the laws of the religion of Islam is forbidden. Someone who lives where he is unable to carry
out his religious obligations must emigrate. If he is unable to do so it is
nevertheless recommendable to leave, but it is not obligatory. To support
an enemy of the Muslims with personal military service or with money is
forbidden. They are under the obligation to avoid doing so with all available means: by going away, resisting, or bribery. If this can only be done by
emigrating, then this emigration is a personal obligation."

How to Judge Muslim Soldiers Who Refuse Service in the Army of the Mongols?

If his service is useful to Muslims, and he is able to bear it, then he should
not leave his post unless his desertion befits Muslims. However, for him to
be in the forefront during the jihad is better than voluntary acts of worship
like prayer, pilgrimage, and fasting.

How to Judge Fighting Them?

The leading scholars of Islam agree that a group of people who refuse to
carry out part of the clear and reliably transmitted duties of Islam have to
be fought.

    The pious forefathers and the leading authoritative imams have always
agreed that these people have to be fought. The first one who did so was
Caliph 'Ali ibn Abu Pith. All through the Umayyad and Abbasid caliph-
ates Muslim army commanders have continued to do so, even when they
were unjust (and not good Muslims). All Muslim imams commanded
us to fight these Mongols, and their likes—the equivalent of our rulers
today—are even more rebellious against the laws of Islam than those who
refused the *zakat* tax. Whosoever doubts they should be fought is ignorant
of the religion of Islam.

Is to Fight Them the Same as Fighting the Rebels?

Ibn Taymiyah says, "Whosoever is killed is a martyr even when his possessions are left intact; whosoever is killed is a martyr even when he did not personally participate in the battle; whosoever is killed is a martyr even when his family is saved from the enemy." If this is so, how much more justified are we to fight people who rebel against the prescripts of Islam and who fight God and his Apostle?

Ideas and Misunderstandings

In the Islamic world there are several ideas about the elimination of these rulers and the establishment of the rule of God—exalted and majestic he is. To what extent are these ideas correct?

Benevolent Societies
There are those who say that we should establish societies that are subject to the state and that urge people to perform their prayers and pay their *zakat* tax and do other good works. These are duties that we should not neglect. However, when we ask ourselves, "Do these works bring about the establishment of an Islamic state?" then the immediate answer must be "No."

Obedience, Education, and Abundance of Acts of Devotion
There are those who say that we should occupy ourselves with obedience to God, with educating the Muslims, and with exerting ourselves in acts of devotion, because the backwardness in which we live is on account of our sins.

Whoever thinks that this abrogates the duty of jihad destroys himself and those who listen to him. Whoever really wants to occupy the highest degree of obedience and wants to reach the peak of devotion must commit himself to jihad for the cause of God.

The truth is that whoever adheres to the philosophy of devoting himself only to acts of devotion is a coward.

The Foundation of a Political Party
There are those who say that we must establish an Islamic political, with the aim of destroying the infidel state and replacing it with an Islamic

one. To work with a political party will, however, have the opposite effect, since it means working within and collaborating with the pagan state.

Nonviolent Propaganda

Some of them say that the right road to the establishment of an Islamic state is nonviolent propaganda and the creation of a broad base. This, however, will not bring about the creation of an Islamic state. Islam does not triumph by attracting the support of the majority.

Nonviolent propaganda cannot be successful because the means of communication today are under the control of the wicked state or under the control of those who are at war with God's religion. The only effective method would be to liberate the media from the control of these people through a convincing victory.

To Be Occupied with the Quest for Knowledge

There are some who say that at present the true road is the quest for knowledge. "How can we fight when we have no knowledge of Islam and its prescripts?" But we shall not heed the words of someone who permits the neglect of a religious command or one of the duties of Islam for the sake of knowledge, certainly not if this duty is the duty of jihad. How can someone who has specialized in [Islamic] religious studies and who really knows all about small and great sins not have noticed the great importance of jihad and the punishment for postponing or neglecting it?

Scholarship is not the decisive weapon that will put an end to paganism. This can only be done with the weapon that the Lord mentioned in his word: "Fight them and God will punish them at your hands, will humiliate them and aid you against them, and will bring healing to the breasts of people who are believers." We do not have a low opinion of the importance of scholarship. On the contrary, we emphasize its importance. We do not, however, excuse ourselves by appealing to the need for scholarship from carrying out the obligations that God prescribed.

Revolt against the Ruler

Reliable tradition says, and the leading Muslim scholars agree, that the duties of leadership cannot be given to an infidel, and that when a leader suddenly becomes an unbeliever, his leadership comes to an end. The same is the case when he neglects to perform the prayer ceremonies, or to urge others to perform them. When he suddenly becomes an unbeliever, or changes God's law, or introduces an innovation, he no longer qualifies as a leader. It is no longer a duty to obey him, and Muslims have the duty to revolt and depose him.

The Enemy Who Is Near and the Enemy Who Is Far

It is said that the battlefield of jihad today is the liberation of Jerusalem. It is true that the liberation of the Holy Land is a religious command, obligatory for all Muslims, but the Prophet described the believer as "sagacious and prudent," and this means that a Muslim knows what is useful and what is harmful and gives priority to definitive solutions. This is a point that makes the explanation of the following necessary.

1. First, to fight an enemy who is near is more important than to fight an enemy who is far.
2. Second, Muslim blood will be shed in order to realize this victory. So it must be asked, Will this victory benefit Muslims or the infidel state? We must beware of fighting for a ruler's nationalist goals that only appear to be Islamic goals.
3. Third, to begin by putting an end to imperialism is not laudatory and not useful. It a waste of time. We must concentrate on our own Islamic situation. We have to establish the rule of God's religion in our own country first and then make the word of God supreme. There is no doubt the first battlefield of the Islamic jihad is to replace our infidel rulers.

The Answer to Those Who Say That Islam Is Defensive Only

It is proper to refute those who say that jihad in Islam is defensive, and that Islam was not spread by the sword. This is a false view, which is nevertheless repeated by a great number of Islamic missionaries. The right answer comes from the Prophet when he was asked: "What is jihad for God's cause?" He then said: "Whosoever fights in order to make the Word of God supreme is someone who fights for God's cause." Islam fights to make supreme the Word of God in this world, whether it be by attacking or by defending.

Islam Spread by the Sword

It is obligatory for the Muslims to raise their swords under the very eyes of the leaders who hide the truth and spread falsehoods. If (Muslims) do not do this, the truth will not reach the hearts of men.

The Verse of the Sword

Most Qur'an commentators have said something about a certain verse from the Qur'an which they have named the "Verse of the Sword" (Qur'an 9.5):

> Then when the sacred months have slipped away, slay the unbelievers wherever ye find them, seize them, beset them, lie in ambush for them everywhere.

Al-Ufi said about this verse, "No contract, nor covenant of protection, was left to a single infidel since this dissolution of treaty obligations was revealed."

The Qur'an scholar Muhammad ibn Ahmad says, "The abrogation of the command to be at peace with the infidels, to forgive them, to be passively exposed to them and to endure their insults preceded here the command to fight them. This makes it superfluous to repeat the abrogation of the command to live in peace with the infidels at each Qur'anic passage. Commands to live in peace with them, which are found in 114 verses in 54 surahs are all abrogated by his word: "Slay the polytheists wherever ye find them."

> So when you meet those who have disbelieved, let there be slaughter. (Qur'an 47.4)

Fighting Is Now a Duty upon All Muslims

The question now is: When is jihad an individual duty? Jihad becomes an individual duty in three situations:

1. First, when two armies meet and their ranks are facing each other, it is forbidden to those who are present to leave, and it becomes an individual duty to remain standing.

2. Second, when the infidels descend upon a country, it becomes an individual duty for its people to fight them and drive them away.
3. Third, when the Imam calls upon a people to fight, they must depart into battle.

With regard to the lands of Islam, the enemy lives right in the middle of them. The enemy even has got hold of the reins of power, for this enemy is the rulers who have seized the leadership of the Muslims. Therefore, waging jihad against them is an individual duty.

Know that when jihad is an individual duty, there is no requirement to ask permission of parents to wage jihad.

The Aspects of Jihad Are Not Successive Phases of Jihad

It is clear that today jihad is an individual duty of every Muslim. Nevertheless, we find that there are those who argue that they need to educate their own souls, and that jihad has successive phases. Imam Ibn Qayyim distinguished three aspects in jihad:

1. Jihad against one's own soul
2. Jihad against the Devil
3. Jihad against the infidels and the hypocrites

This argument shows either complete ignorance or excessive cowardice, because Ibn Qayyim only distinguished *aspects* in jihad, he did not divide it into successive phases. Otherwise we would have to suspend the waging of jihad against the Devil until we finished the phase of jihad against our own soul.

Whoever studies the life of Muhammad will find that whenever jihad was proclaimed, everybody rushed off for God's cause, even perpetrators of great sins and those who had only recently adopted Islam.

The jihad against the soul is a fabricated tradition, and the only reason for inventing it is to reduce the value of fighting with the sword so as to distract the Muslims from fighting the infidels and the hypocrites.

Fear of Failure

It is said that we fear to establish the state [because] after one or two days a reaction will occur that will put to an end everything we have accomplished.

The refutation of this view is that the establishment of an Islamic state is the execution of a divine command. We are not responsible for its results. Someone who is so stupid as to hold this view, which has no use except to hinder Muslims from the execution of their religious duty by establishing the rule of God, forgets that when the rule of the infidel has fallen, everything will be in the hands of the Muslims, whereupon the downfall of the Islamic state will become inconceivable.

This is God's promise: when the hypocrites see that the power is in the ranks of Islam, they will come back in submission, so we will not be deceived by these voices that will quickly fade away and be extinguished.

Incitement to Jihad for the Cause of God

A Muslim has the duty to prepare himself for jihad for God's cause only. If you fight jihad for God, he guarantees that you will either enter paradise or come back to your home with whatever booty he obtained. There is no disagreement on the reliability of this tradition.

The Prophet says, "Whoever truthfully asks for martyrdom will be put in the (heavenly) abodes of the martyrs even if he dies in his bed."

"Once a man came to the Apostle of God and said to him: 'Show me a work which equals jihad.' The Apostle of God answered: 'There is none.'"

The Prophet says, "A martyr has six virtues in the eyes of God."

1. He will be forgiven upon the first drop of blood.
2. His seat will be in paradise.
3. He will be free from the punishment of the grave.
4. He will be dressed in the garb of faith.
5. He will marry the heavenly dark-eyed virgins.
6. He will intercede for 70 of his relatives.

The Punishment for Neglecting Jihad

Neglecting jihad is the cause of the lowness, humiliation, division, and fragmentation in which Muslims live today.

The Prophet says, "When people yearn for money and wealth and conclude their bargains upon credit, and neglect to participate in jihad, then a Plague from Heaven will be sent upon them, and this Plague will not be lifted from them until they turn back to their religion."

A Muslim must not be content today to be in the ranks of women.

Legal Difficulties and Their Refutation

There are some who fear to enter into this kind of fighting, arguing that those with whom we will be confronted have armies that include both Muslims and infidels. So how can we fight the Muslims?

We cannot know who are the ones who were forced into the army of the infidels. We cannot differentiate between those who are and those who are not. When we kill them in accordance with the command of God, we are both rewarded and excused. They, however, will be judged according to their intentions. Whoever is forced into an army of infidels is not able to withdraw from fighting. He will be reunited with his fellow Muslims on the Day of Resurrection.

The Proper Method of Fighting

There is no doubt that the modern methods of fighting differ to a certain extent from the methods of fighting in the time of the Prophet—what is the Muslim's method of fighting in this day and age? Can he use his own intellect and his own individual judgment?

Deceiving the Infidels: One of the Arts of Fighting in Islam

The Prophet says: "War is deceit." Scholars are agreed on the permissibility of deceiving the infidels in war however possible, except when this would imply a breach of a treaty or of a promise of safety. It is, however, a fact that there is no treaty between us and them since they wage war against the religion of God, and therefore Muslims are free to choose the most suitable method of fighting so that deception, which is victory with the fewest losses and by the easiest means possible, is realized.

The Method of Fighting in the Attack of the Ahzab

After the Jewish leaders were successful in inciting unbelieving groups against the Prophet, the situation became dangerous and Muslims quickly conceived a unique plan to dig a deep trench that would encircle Medina from the side of the plain and make a division between the defenders and the attackers. Thus the method chosen for fighting is not a revelation, nor is it an established custom. Therefore the Muslim has the right to use his own intellect, to organize, and to deliberate.

Lying to the Enemy

The permissibility of lying is clear from the tradition. Al-Tabari said: "In respect to lying in war, oblique modes of speech are permitted, that is, without in fact lying, which is not allowed."

Islamic Planning

By studying the night expeditions, wherein the Muslims marched at night and lay in concealment during the day, Muslims can extract Islamic plans and battle deceptions whose principles were practiced by many Muslims.

An Important Point

Ibn Taymiyah says that it is permissible for a Muslim to penetrate into the ranks [spies] of the infidel army, even though this will lead to his death before he can see with his own eyes the advantage of this penetration.

There Are Those Who Have Distanced Themselves from the Right Path

People who refuse to wage jihad are those who shirk hardship and flee from effort, and prefer cheap comfort to noble toil, base safety to sweet danger, and they collapse exhausted behind the marching fighting ranks who are in earnest, knowing the burdens of missions that serve to further the cause of Islam. These fighting ranks remain on their path, which is filled with obstacles and thorns, because they are aware with an innate knowledge that fighting the obstacles and thorns is natural to man and that it is more pleasant and more beautiful than sitting and staying behind.

These are the people who prefer comfort to struggle in the hour of difficulty and these people are not suited for strife. Their participation in jihad is not hoped for, nor is it allowed to force them to participate. The glory of jihad should not be given to these people who stayed behind and did so willingly.

Missions that further the cause of Islam require solid, straightforward, steady, and healthy constitutions that can withstand a long and difficult strife. Military ranks that are permeated with the weak and the soft cannot effectively resist because these weaklings will abandon the ranks in the hour of difficulty. They will cause failure, weakness, and confusion to spread through the ranks. It is necessary to banish those who are weak in order to protect these from being put to flight. Indulgence toward those weak people is a crime toward the whole army.

CHAPTER 5
The Management of Savagery

ABU BAKR NAJI

Naji's identity is unknown. Some Islamist writers have said that he was Tunisian, but a Saudi newspaper identified him as Jordanian. Will McCants, a West Point scholar who has translated the entirety of Naji's work, claims that he might be a pseudonym for several different theorists of jihad. But he adds that Naji's work has appeared on Sawt al-Jihad, *the authoritative al Qaida Internet magazine, meaning that it reflects the prevailing views of the organization.*

Naji's work appeared in 2004 and quickly spread throughout the jihadist community. It advocates the continual attack on the vital economic centers of enemies, particularly those of weak countries. Naji's assumption is that eventually these attacks will so cripple a nation's government that it will lose control of whole regions and that these regions will descend into a state of savagery. He believes that if these savage regions are managed correctly by radial Islamist cadres, they will provide strong and secure bases for the spread of global jihad.

Introduction

The management of savagery is the next stage that the *ummah* will pass through and it is a stage that will be a bridge to the Islamic state, which has been awaited since the fall of the caliphate. If we fail, it does not mean the end of the matter; rather, this failure will lead to an increase in savagery! This increase in savagery, which may result from failure, is not the worst thing that can happen. Rather, the most abominable of the levels of savagery is still less than stability under the order of unbelief by several degrees.

Preface

The two superpowers that used to dominate the global order controlled it through their centralized power. The meaning of "centralized power" here is: the overwhelming military power that extends from the center in order to control the areas of land that submit to each superpower, beginning from the center and reaching the utmost extremity of these lands.

There is no doubt that the power God gave to the two superpowers (America and Russia) was overwhelming. However, in reality, using pure, human reason, one understands that this power is not able to impose its authority from the center upon lands in Egypt and Yemen unless these countries submit to those powers entirely of their own accord. Therefore, the two superpowers must resort to using a deceptive media halo that portrays these powers as noncoercive and world-encompassing, able to reach into every earth and heaven.

When a state submits to the illusion of the deceptive power and behaves on this basis, that is when its downfall begins. It is just as the American author Paul Kennedy says: "If America expands the use of its military power and strategically extends more than necessary, this will lead to its downfall."

Overwhelming military power may become a curse to this great superpower if the cohesion of society collapses. Several elements that cause this collapse are the corruption of religion, moral collapse, social iniquities, opulence, selfishness, giving priority to worldly pleasures, and the love of the world over all values. Whenever a large mixture of these elements are combined within the superpower, that superpower's speed of collapse increases. Whether these elements are actively present or latent, they need an assisting element to activate them and cause the downfall of that superpower.

This is exactly what happened to the Communist superpower when it was put in a military confrontation with a power weaker than itself by several degrees. However, the weaker power succeeded in exhausting it militarily and, even more important, it activated the elements of cultural annihilation in the superpower's homeland:

- The dogma of atheism versus belief systems that believe in the next life and a God.
- Love of the world, worldly pleasures, and opulence versus individuals who had nothing to lose.
- Moral corruption, the least manifestation of which was that Russian soldiers or officers returned home—if they returned—and found that their wives had a child or relationship with someone else.
- Social iniquities clearly floated to the surface when the economic situation weakened because of the war. Then when money becomes scarce and monetary crises begin, the major thieves appear.

Additionally, note that the economic weakness resulting from the burdens of war is the most important element of cultural annihilation since it threatens the opulence and worldly pleasures that those societies thirst for. Then competition for these things begins after they grow scarce due to the weakness of the economy. Likewise, social iniquities rise to the surface on account of the economic stagnation, which ignites political opposition and disunity among the various sectors of society. However, this weak force acted upon a special emotion in the *ummah*. It revived the dogma of jihad in the hearts of the Muslim masses—who had submitted to the superpower. When they saw the example and model of these poor, Afghani people—their neighbors in jihad—it helped them to remain steadfast in the face of the strongest military arsenal and the most vicious army in the world. Thus we saw that the jihad brought forth many Muslims from unknown lands, like Chechnya and Tajikistan. Sheikh 'Abd Allah 'Azzam—who was martyred before the fall of the Soviet Union—had an analysis that predicted the fall of this superpower and the emergence of Islamic movements that would oppose some of its republics. Even more remarkable than this is that his analysis was built on numbers, such that he calculated the number of the forces of the Russian army, which possessed a great arsenal of weapons in the world, unparallel viciousness, and the ability to endure battles and human losses. It depended on the idea that pressure from the mujahideen would push Russia to pump larger numbers of troops into Afghanistan, which would reduce the reserves of the Soviet army, and that this pressure and reduction would encourage the Soviet republics to try to secede, especially the Islamic republics.

Almost everything he said happened, as if it were a cinematic film. From this we know that understanding the abilities of the enemy and the time of his defeat only comes to us by plunging into active war with him, regardless of whether we have a rational mind or theoretical research at hand.

The superpower's republics fell into chaos when it collapsed. But because new governments quickly came into existence, administration was established in most of them without passing through the stage of savagery.

In Chechnya and Afghanistan, however, the administrations of savagery succeeded in establishing what can be called states, but they have collapsed now. They have returned to a stage before the administration of savagery, which is the stage of exhaustion. We also note that the course of events in the two countries is not due to momentous events of September 11, even if they perhaps hastened it.

So that superpower collapsed, but the civilization of Satan was able to quickly rectify the matter and stabilize control in the world through the cohesion of the remaining power—America. The picture became even bleaker in the eyes of some of the noble people—whether they are religious or otherwise as states submitted to America's global order. They doubt that the remaining superpower can be annihilated and that the components of its power differ in kind from the collapsed superpower, especially since its media halo is much stronger.

O people! The viciousness of the Russian soldier is double that of the American soldier. If the number of Americans killed is one-tenth of the number of Russians killed in Afghanistan and Chechnya, they will flee, heedless of all else. That is because the current structure of the American and Western military is not the same as the structure of their military in the era of colonialism. They reached a stage of effeminacy that made them unable to sustain battles for a long period of time, and they compensate for this with a deceptive media halo.

The contemporary renewal movement was purified after momentous events and battles severely damaged it and it accumulated experience during more than thirty years. It must now undertake specific operations arranged systematically and carry out what began with the operation of Nairobi and Dar al-Salam for the achievement of the following goals:

A—The first goal: Destroy a large part of the respect for America and spread confidence in the souls of Muslims by means of:

(1) Reveal the deceptive media to be a power without force.

(2) Force America to abandon its war against Islam by proxy and force it to attack directly so that the noble ones among the masses and a few of the noble ones among the armies of apostasy will see that their fear of deposing the regimes because America is their protector is misplaced.

B—The second goal: Replace the human casualties sustained by the renewal movement during the past thirty years by means of the human aid that will probably come for two reasons:

(1) Being dazzled by the operations that will be undertaken in opposition to America.

(2) Anger over the obvious, direct American interference in the Islamic world, such that that anger compounds the previous anger against America's support for the Zionist entity.

C—The third goal: Work to expose the weakness of America's centralized power. As a result, the apostates among all of the sects and groups and even Americans themselves will see that the remoteness of the primary center from the peripheries is a major factor contributing to the possible outbreak of chaos and savagery.

Definition of "The Management of Savagery"

The management of savagery is defined very succinctly as the management of savage chaos! This management will work through several phases:

1. Managing the people's needs with regard to food and medical treatment.
2. Being responsible for offering services like education and so forth.
3. The preservation of security and securing the borders.
4. Working to expand the region of savagery.

Before its submission to the administration, the region of savagery will be in a situation resembling the situation of Afghanistan before the control of the Taliban, a region submitting to the law of the jungle, whose good people yearn for someone to manage this savagery. They even accept any organization, regardless of whether it is made up of good or evil people. However, if the evil people manage this savagery, it is possible that this region will become even more barbarous!

Before we proceed to another point, we want to clarify the requirements of the management of savagery in the ideal form we desire. These requirements are:

- Spreading internal security.
- Providing food and medical treatment.
- Securing the region of savagery from the invasions of enemies.
- Establishing sharia justice among the people who live in the regions of savagery.
- Raising the level of belief and combat efficiency during the training of the youth of the region of savagery and establishing a fighting society at all levels and among all individuals.
- Working for the spread of sharia science.
- Dissemination of spies and seeking to complete the construction of a minimal intelligence agency.
- Uniting the hearts of the world's people by means of money and uniting the world through sharia governance.
- Deterring the hypocrites with proof and other means and forcing them to repress and conceal their hypocrisy, to hide their discouraged opinions, and to comply with those in authority until their evil is put in check.
- Progressing until it is possible to expand and attack the enemies in order to repel them, plunder their money, and place them in a constant state of apprehension.

During the modern age it became difficult to establish administrations to control savagery because of the consolidation of the *jahili* control over the world through racist regimes, financial control, and borders enclosing so-called states of the world. Nevertheless, several administrations of savagery were established, especially in places that are remote from the center of power. Among these were the groups fighting in Afghanistan and the first stages of the Taliban movement until it established its state—may God restore it in power and loftiness. Likewise, there is the Abu Sayyaf movement and the Moro Liberation Front in the Philippines, and the jihad movements in Algeria during some periods of jihad in the 1990s. Similarly, there are the Islamic groups and others in Somalia after the fall of the state of Siyad Bare. We do not think that movements like Hamas and Islamic Jihad in Palestine currently, or the Islamic Group in Egypt in the 1990s, and other similar groups are administrating barbarous areas. Rather, they were, and still are, in a stage that precedes the administration of savagery, which is a stage called the "stage of the power of vexation and exhaustion." It is the stage that usually precedes the stage of the

administration of savagery, when the person undertaking "vexation" cal-
culates that savagery will happen and prepares for its administration.

The Path for Establishing an Islamic State

Stages
- The stage of "the power of vexation and exhaustion."
- The stage of "the administration of savagery."
- The stage of "the establishment of power—establishing the state."
- Stages of the remaining states.

States Designated as Part of the Priority Group
Recent studies of the renewal movement have designated a group of states
that the mujahideen should focus on so that their striking power will not
be dissipated in states where results may be minimal; however, there is
flexibility in the selection according to developments. These studies were
distributed in the three years prior to the momentous events of September.
After these events and the developments that followed them, the leadership announced some modifications and excluded some of the regions from
the group of priority regions. They also added two additional regions—
the countries of the Haramayn [Mecca and Medina—Saudi Arabia] and
Nigeria. Thus the states initially designated for inclusion in the group of
priority regions are:

Jordan, the Maghrib, Nigeria, Pakistan, Haramayn, Yemen.

This selection is preliminary, of course. However, the people of each
of these regions should carefully contemplate the possibility of whether or
not they can move in a centralized way to assist the jihad.

Factors Considered When Selecting Countries
With regard to the common links between states in which the regions of
savagery can come into being, we notice that some or all of the following
factors pertain to them:
- The presence of geographical depth and topography permits.
- The weakness of the ruling regime and the weakness of the centraliza-
  tion of its power in the peripheries of the borders of its state and sometimes in internal regions, particularly those that are overcrowded.

- The presence of jihadists, Islamic expansion being propagated in these regions.
- The nature of the people in these regions. This is a matter in which God has given preference to one place over another.
- Likewise, the distribution of weapons by people who are in those regions.

Among the happy twists of fate, by the permission of God, is that most of the priority countries are in remote areas, a fact that makes it difficult for any state powers to control the wide region at the heart of the Islamic world.

As for the remaining regions of the Islamic world, they suffer from the power of their ruling regimes, and the lack of regions whose geographical features permit the freedom of movement found in the priority regions. However, these regions must begin with "vexation" operations, which have actually begun in Turkey, Tunisia, and other places.

In summary, the stage of the "power of vexation and exhaustion" by means of groups and separate cells in every region of the Islamic world should continue until the anticipated chaos and savagery breaks out in several priority regions, in accordance with the studies. In the meantime, chaos will not happen in the regions of the remaining states due to the power of the regimes within them. Then the regions of chaos and savagery will advance to the stage of the administration of savagery, while the remaining regions and states of the Islamic world will continue on two flanks—the flank of logistical support for regions of savagery controlled by us and the flank of the "power of vexation and exhaustion" directed against their regimes, until victory comes to it from outside. By logistical support, I mean money, a place for transferring people (i.e., safe houses), sheltering of components, the media, and so on.

The Primary Goals for the Stage of the "Power of Vexation and Exhaustion"

1. Exhausting the forces of the enemy and the regimes collaborating with them, dispersing their efforts, and working to make them unable to catch their breath by means of operations in the regions of the choice states, primary or otherwise, even if the operations are small in size or effect. Although the blow of the rod may only strike a (single)

Crusader head, its spread and escalation will have an effect for a long period of time.

2. Attracting new youth to the jihadist work by undertaking quality operations that will grab people's attention. By "qualitative operations," I mean qualitative, medium operations like the operation in Bali, the operation in Riyadh, the operations in Turkey, and the large operations in Iraq. I do not mean qualitative operations like the operation of September. Thinking too much about doing something like the latter might impede the undertaking of qualitative operations that are smaller in size. Moreover, if there is an opportunity for doing something like it, it is better not to do so in haste without knowing the opinion of the High Command.

3. Dislodging the chosen regions—removing the control of the local regimes over the area we have decided will be our priority effort.

4. The fourth goal of the stage of "the power of vexation and exhaustion" is the advancement of groups of vexation through drilling and operational practice so that they will be prepared psychologically and practically for the stage of the management of savagery.

The Plan of Action and Movement

We launched sequential strikes against America, ending with the strike of September, which America deserved according to the sharia. Likewise, all future strikes will succeed if they are faithfully discharged. The inevitable result of this escalating sequence is the fall of the prestige of America among the masses and among the elites of the world in the armies of apostasy.

As a consequence, America will either seek revenge and the conflict will intensify or it will launch a limited war. In the case of the latter, its grudge will not be satisfied and it will not succeed in curbing this escalating expansion. America might have caused the downfall of the state of Afghanistan, which it had already planned for. However, America will begin to confront the transformation of this expansion into tens of thousands of groups like those of September, which will turn their strikes against it, and America will not find a state as an entity from which it can take its revenge. Thus it will become clear to it that the regimes that support it cannot protect it from attacks and cannot preserve its strategic interests and the interests of its adopted daughter, Israel, in the region. It has no choice but to fall into the second trap. As for the first trap, we have already mentioned it. It is the invasion of Afghanistan. The mere failure of America to achieve all of its military goals in this country and the continuing resistance of this country throughout two years or more will convince the masses and some of the noble ones among the armies of apostasy that opposition to America is possible. As for the second trap, it is to put America's armies, which occupy the region, in a state of war with the masses in the region. It is obvious at this very moment that it stirs up movements that increase the jihadist expansion and create legions among the youth who contemplate and plan for resistance. Behold the blows that are directed toward America and its allies in both the East and the West! These blows have continued until this very moment. Therefore, what is the plan by which we shall shape events from now until we have completely accomplished our goals, which we mentioned above? We must diversify and widen the vexation strikes against the Crusader-Zionist enemy in every place in the Islamic world, and even outside of it if possible, so as to disperse the efforts of the enemy. For example: If a tourist resort that the Crusaders patronize in Indonesia is hit, all of the tourist resorts in all of the states of the world will have to be secured by additional forces. If a usurious bank belonging to the Crusaders is struck in Turkey, all of the banks belonging to the Crusaders will have to be secured in all countries, causing a great economic drain. If an oil interest is hit near the port of Aden, there will have to be intensive security measures put in place for all of the oil companies.

The Targets We Must Concentrate on and the Reasons for That

We said that we should strike any kind of target permitted in the sharia. However, it is necessary to focus on economic targets, particularly petroleum. The reason for doing so is that this is the core of the enemy and its great leaders will only be cut down by this means. Hitting economic targets will force the enemy to goad the regimes, which are already exhausted from protecting other targets, into pumping in more forces for economic protection. As a result, feebleness will start to appear in their forces, especially since their forces are limited. Often, large numbers of troops are structurally weak and it is easy to attack them and take large amounts of their weapons. Moreover, the public will see how the troops flee. At this point, savagery and chaos begin and these regions will start to suffer from the absence of security. At the occurrence of savagery: If our groups are close to the place of savagery or there is a way to get to it and there are spies and individuals in the region of savagery who will give their allegiance to us, then we must study the situation and the extent of our capacity to settle there. If some of the groups of vexation unite in a single entity and settle there in order to manage one of the regions of savagery, it must, along with the regions of savagery neighboring it, balance between concentrating in one place and spreading out, so that the enemy will feel uneasy. This will frighten the leaders, while their subordinates begin to think about uniting with the mujahideen in order to die as martyrs rather than dying with the tyrannical infidels. At this point the enemy may lean toward reconciliation and the enemy will satisfy himself with retreating to the back lines for the protection of the economy, and this is where his troops will be concentrated. With the return of the enemy to the back lines, he withdraws from positions and security breaks down and savagery increases. Furthermore, the mujahideen begin to complete their development, following up, training, and achieving the next steps. Thus the reputation and stature of the mujahideen begin to rise.

Whenever the enemy sees this spirit, he can do nothing but unite with the mujahideen or withdraw even more. An increase of savagery also results, which we must manage after we have studied the region where it occurs and communicated with our vanguards in it.

Simplifying the Preceding Plan on Specific Points

This plan requires:
- A military strategy working to disperse the efforts and forces of the enemy and to exhaust and drain its monetary and military capabilities.
- A media strategy targeting and focusing on two classes. The first class is the masses, in order to push a large number of them to join the jihad, offer positive support, and adopt a negative attitude toward those who do not join the ranks. The second class is the troops of the enemy who have low salaries, in order to push them to join the ranks of the mujahideen or at least to flee from the service of the enemy.

After a suitable period of time, we will work for:
- Developing a military strategy in order to push the forces of the enemy to pull back around the economic targets in order to protect them.

- Developing the media strategy such that it reaches and targets the heart of the middle leadership of the armies of apostasy in order to push them to join the jihad.
- Planning, preparing, and training for the exploitation of the results of the previous points—the outbreak of chaos and savagery.
- Establishing a media plan that seeks, in each of these stages, rational and sharia justification for the operations, especially targeting the masses. However, the masses are a difficult factor, but will be our backbone in the future, provided that there is transparency in our plans and we are not slow to acknowledge errors—sometimes.

Notice that when we say that the masses are the difficult factor, our meaning is not that we make our movement dependent on them. We know that they are not generally dependable. We also know that there is no improvement for the general public until there is victory. However, it has been decreed that the people are a reserve capable of effective action. On the assumption that we need half a million mujahideen for our long battle until it ends as we wish, the possibility of adding this number from a nation of one billion people is easier than adding them from the youth of the Islamic movement who are polluted by the doubts of the evil sheikhs.

Mastery of the Art of Management

By the grace of God, organized Islamic work is beginning to be managed at the highest administrative level, especially the jihadist organizations. However, there still needs to be more mastery of techniques and general training, especially since we are approaching a stage in which our administrative needs will be expanded to handle the administration of savagery. Here we will mix with hundreds of thousands of people requiring administration of their regions from us as diminished governments. If we are not prepared to deal with that, we will face dangerous problems.

The most important skill of the art of administration is learning how to establish committees and dividing labor so that all activities do not fall on the shoulders of a single person or small group of people. It is necessary that each individual be trained in all or a large part of the branches so that it is possible to pass on skills, according to need, from one place to another. Of course, this is without the individuals knowing the secrets of the branches in which they do not work; rather, I mean training and passing on practical knowledge.

It is possible to discover individuals within each group who have mastered the art of administration innately. However, the urgent need remains to polish these talents through acquired learning and practical exercise. Naturally, in the beginning those with previous experience will advance, and they must undertake the preparation of the second generation. The most prominent of those who have been selected among the second generation are the intelligent, pious students of Islamic knowledge, and those who responded to horrors and calamities with composure, calmness, and deep thought. We must make use of books on the subject of administration, especially the management studies and theories that have been recently published, since they are consonant with the nature of modern societies. There is more than one site on the Internet in which one can obtain management books. I believe that the tomes that can be downloaded from the site "The Notebook of Islam" are very good, especially since they include tomes of modern global studies. Likewise, the commentaries provide ample warning against sharia mistakes.

Who Leads, Who Manages, and Who Authorizes the Fundamental Administrative Decisions?

There is a dependable rule in Islamic activism, which is, "Not every leader is a manager and not every manager is a leader." If we were to abide by what we mentioned in the previous point, we should change this phrase into "Every leader is a manager but not every manager is a leader." The manager or executive is any individual within the movement or the group—who has mastered the art of administration—who can be appointed to manage a financial or nutritional sector or the like without him knowing, to the extent possible, the secrets that would harm the work. And as for the leader, he must be the object of complete reliance within the movement and entrusted with its actions and its secrets. The leaders no doubt know many of the secrets of the movement to the same extent. Some of the leaders issue fundamental and secondary administrative decisions, while others issue decisions that include sharia dimensions. Therefore, in our plan we open the door of management wide to those who have mastered its art. As for the door of leadership, it is only open to those who are reliable, even though there is a security apparatus that keeps watch over the two doors, monitoring the professionalism of the actions of the leaders and the managers in order to prevent infiltration.

Using the Time-Tested Principles of Military Combat

Wisdom is the goal of the believer, and even if we generally follow in the footsteps of the Prophet and his companions, we only accept that our policies in any jihadist action are sharia policies, unless the sharia permits us to use the plans and military principles of non-Muslims in which there is no sin.

Regrettably, some of the small groups in the previous stages of jihad ignored these military principles not out of fear of contradicting the sharia. This error was facilitated by random behavior and rigidity, along with the desire of the praiseworthy youths to attain unto the station of martyrdom as soon as possible. Anything that pushes these groups toward the benefit of acting in accordance with intellectual military principles will be a major step toward achieving the goals.

Following the time-tested principles of military combat will shorten for us the long years in which we might suffer the corrupting influences of rigidity and random behavior. Truly, abandoning random behavior and implementing military science will facilitate our achievement of stated goals and enable us to improve the execution of our plans.

The teaching of these principles opens a wide vista for creativity; and perhaps extraordinary leaders will emerge who will write their theories in books of modern history. Here I will mention some examples related to a few of the principles in order to sharpen the mind and clarify the importance of following them in order to improve the efficacy of our military actions:

1. There is an important principle that states, "If regular armies concentrate in one place they lose control. Conversely, if they spread out, they lose effectiveness." The meaning of the first half of the principle is that when we target something, it is impossible for the enemy to put massive amounts of forces in this place. And if they do, they will lose control when the first shot is fired and their forces will hit each other. Therefore, the enemy will put in place forces that are commensurate with the nature and size of the location. Thus we must know the nature and types of locations in which the size of the enemy's forces enables us to prepare a force to attack it, because it is impos-

sible for the enemy to increase its forces within it. Likewise, we learn, in the first half of the principle, of the importance of learning the art of choosing the location of the clash with the enemy under any time or circumstances when a clash is imposed upon us. As for the second half of the principle, it is the most important and has an effect on the first half. The second half states that whenever the forces of the enemy spread out over the largest area of terrain, they lose their effectiveness and attacking them becomes easy. Perhaps this half of the principle is the primary principle that the enlightened among the youths of jihad follow. Likewise, we find that most of those who are ignorant of this portion of the principle fail.

2. The principles of the rate of operations, whether it is escalating, fixed, or undulating. Sometimes our stages have all three of them. The rate of operations escalates in order to send a living, practical message to the people, the masses, and the enemy's low-ranking troops that the power of the mujahideen is on the rise. All of these people are unaware of these principles and the escalation of operations leaves an imprint in their minds and establishes that the mujahideen are continually advancing and the enemy is in retreat and that the fate of the enemy is defeat. Therefore, when we plan our operations, we should begin with small operations and then undertake larger ones, and so forth—even if we are capable of undertaking the largest operations from the very beginning—just as the al Qaida organization arranged operations to ignite confrontation.

3. Also among the important principles is a principle that is beneficial as a general strategy and also beneficial for planning small operations. This principle states: "Strike with your striking force multiple times and with the maximum power you possess in the most locations."

It is worth pointing out here how the High Command used to consider the youth of the Arabian Peninsula as their striking force, but it did not select the peninsula for change due to factors mentioned in previous studies and on account of the momentous events of September. However, after the momentous events of September there was a reversal in these factors and the peninsula became one of the selected states. And we even note that the leadership gave it priority because the enemy within it—which is the regime of the Al Saud—is similar to most of the regimes hostile to the mujahideen in its weakness. Thus, the Arabian Peninsula is an ideal place for the application of this principle.

As for applying this principle when planning for small operations, here is an example: An active group made up of ten individuals is facing a very simple operation—a nonmartyrdom operation, of course—and this operation only needs one or two individuals. The group will sometimes even send a single mujahid or two for a larger operation. However, if it sends all of its members on this secure operation for the purpose of massacring and terrorizing the enemy, when the people and the newspapers talk about what happened, they will think that the coming operations will be even more concentrated and have a commensurate numerical increase, which will raise the reputation of the mujahideen in the media and dissuade hearts from opposing them. However, this principle can only be applied after thorough study of the possibilities and the benefits and drawbacks of doing so. Restricting the number of people for the operation to what is sufficient for carrying it out generally has priority.

Likewise, this principle has other areas of application under different circumstances and exigencies, as is the case with most of the principles. For example, there is a target that is easy to strike, like a building belonging to the enemy in which meetings are held and so forth, and it is destroyed with a small booby trap, even though we have a good cache of explosives that had not been used during our activities. In this case, it is possible to use a quantity of explosives that not only destroys the building or even levels it to the earth; it makes the earth completely swallow it up. By doing so, the amount of the enemy's fear is multiplied and good media goals are achieved, the most prominent of which is the enemy's inability to conceal its losses. Similar operations have to be repeated over and over, and a number of good results will be achieved as a consequence.

4. Another important principle that was one of the pillars of wars in the past and nowadays and that strategists and historians still say the groups of jihad concentrate on in order to hasten the collapse of all of their enemies is, "The most likely way to defeat the strongest enemy militarily is to drain it militarily and economically."

Of course, draining it economically is done primarily by military operations. Even Rumsfeld says to reporters in justification for his setbacks: "What more can we do? Don't forget that we are spending billions in combating an enemy that spends millions." He is right.

All the things that we have mentioned are merely examples and they each pertain to general principles and guidelines. However, the observant person knows that the smallest unit in military operations—even if they were only responsible for the preparation and storing of weapons and cleaning them, for example—submits to rules and regulations that every member must learn. As an appropriate example, I mention here the attempt to assassinate the most vicious leader in Egypt, the minister of information—Safwat al-Sharif. This attempt failed because the one who was supposed to kill him had stored the weapon on the night of the operation in a humid place. When his accomplice who was facing the car shot the guard and his turn came to shoot the minister, the bullets got stuck in the gun and the minister survived.

Among the most important references that we have selected for a good study of the military principles and theories and the arts of war:
- Various encyclopedias of jihad that the mujahideen of Afghanistan have prepared.
- The journal *al-Battar*, which is published out of jihadist military camps in the Arabian Peninsula.
- The writings of Abu 'Ubayd al-Qurashi (may God protect him) in the journal *al-Ansar*. Likewise, other old writings by him and others on the site al-Uswa al-Hasana ("The Beautiful Model").
- General books on the art of war, especially guerrilla wars, as long as the student is able to correct the sharia mistakes that are in them.

Using Violence

Those who study theoretical jihad, meaning they study only jihad as it is written on paper, will never grasp this point well. Regrettably, the youth in our *ummah*, since the time when they were stripped of weapons, no longer understand the nature of wars. One who previously engaged in jihad knows that it is naught but violence, crudeness, terrorism, frightening others, and massacring—I am talking about jihad and fighting, not about Islam, and one should not confuse them. Moreover, he knows that he cannot continue to fight and move from one stage to another unless the beginning stage contains a stage of massacring the enemy and making him homeless. However, there is also often a need for this violence in the other stages. Further, he cannot continue the jihad with softness, whether the softness is in the mode of inviting others to join the jihad, taking up positions, or undertaking operations, since the ingredient of softness is one of the ingredients of failure for any jihadist action. It is better for those who have the intention to begin a jihadist action and are also soft to sit in their homes. If not, failure will be their lot and they will suffer shock afterward. Whoever wants to verify and understand what I mean, he should read biographies and histories and examine what happened to the modern jihadist movement. Regardless of whether we use harshness or softness, our enemies will not be merciful to us if they seize us. Thus it behooves us to make them think one thousand times before attacking us.

If we are not violent in our jihad and if softness seizes us, that will be a major factor in the loss of strength. The *ummah* that possesses strength is the *ummah* that is able to protect the positions it has won and it is the *ummah* that boldly faces horrors and has the firmness of mountains. These are the good qualities that we have lost in this age. The companions understood the matter of violence and they were the best of those who understood this after the prophets. Even the Friend (Abu Bakr) and Ali Abi Talib burned people with fire, even though it is odious, because they knew the effect of rough violence in times of need. The companions were not violent because they loved killing; they were certainly not coarse people. By God! How tender were their hearts! They were the most merciful of creation by nature after the Prophet. However, they understood the nature of unbelief and its people and the nature of a need for severity. We are now in circumstances resembling the circumstances after the death of the Messenger and the outbreak of apostasy that the believers faced in the beginning of the jihad. Thus we need to massacre others. But if God should give us power and we take control and justice spreads, how tender the people of faith will be at that time and they will say to the people: "Go, for you are free."

In addition to this, one should note that violence and coarseness must not transgress the limits of the sharia and that one must pay heed to the benefit and harm that results from it. The sharia considers the rules of jihad as one of the most important subjects for the guidance of creation, if not the most important subject. Pertaining to this, whenever there are reasonable people among the enemy who recognize the truth that every rational mind must assent to, we can lighten the severity of the violence against them. As for the haughty enemy and his troops and his supporters, that is another matter. Among the things connected with the subject of violence is "the policy of paying the price": No harm comes to the *ummah* or to us without the enemy paying a price. Thus in this stage of "the power of vexation and exhaustion," following the strategy of "paying the price" spreads hopelessness in the hearts of the enemy. Any preventative act of any kind against the groups of vexation should be met with a reaction that makes the enemy "pay the price" for his crime so that he will be deterred from doing its like again and think one thousand times before undertaking an attack against us. "Paying the price" must be accomplished even if it is after a long period, even if it is years. The enemy should be reminded of that in a statement justifying the operation of "paying the price," which will make a deep impression on the leaders of the enemy that there is no hostile action they can undertake against Islam and its people, or against the mujahideen for which they, their supporters, or their most powerful institutions will not pay a price over a long or short period of time. On account of that, feelings of hopelessness will creep into the enemy and he will begin to think about leaving the arena on account of this hopelessness and because of his love for the world in the face of generations of mujahideen who will persist in the battle and not be agitated by upheavals but, rather, motivated by them to respond.

As for the stage of "the administration of savagery," we will confront the problem of the aerial attacks of the enemy—crusader or apostate—on military training camps or residential regions in areas that we administer. Even though defensive fortifications and trenches are put in place to deal with that problem, we should also follow the policy of "paying the price" when confronting this crime of the enemy. Thus the enemy will be inclined toward reconciliation, which will enable the regions of savagery to catch their breath and progress. This reconciliation means a temporary stop to fighting without any kind of treaties and concessions. We do not believe in an armistice with the apostate enemy, even if it was brokered with the primary infidel.

Here is an important point: It is best if those who undertake operations of "paying the price" are other groups in other regions against which no hostility has been directed. There are a number of benefits in this, among which the most important is making the enemy feel that he is surrounded and exposed. If the enemy undertakes a hostile action against a region in the Arabian Peninsula or in Iraq, then the response will occur in Morocco or Nigeria or Indonesia. This will cause embarrassment for the enemy, especially if the region in which the operation of "paying the price" occurred submits to the control of the regimes of unbelief or the regimes of apostasy. "Paying the price" is not limited to the Crusader enemy. By way of example, if the apostate Egyptian regime undertakes an action to kill or capture a group of mujahideen, the youth of jihad in Algeria or Morocco can direct a strike against the Egyptian embassy and issue a statement of justification, or they can kidnap Egyptian diplomats as hostages until the group of mujahideen is freed, and so forth. The policy of violence must also be followed such that if the demands are not met, the hostages should be liquidated in a terrifying manner, which will send fear into the hearts of the enemy and his supporters.

Achieving "Power"

"Power" is achieved through ties of religious loyalty. When the enemy knows that if he breaks a portion of a group, the remainder will capitulate, we can say that this group has not achieved "power." But if the enemy knows that if he kills a portion of the group, vengeance for their blood will be undertaken by the remainder, that group has achieved "power" that the enemy fears, especially if the organization of the group is hard to destroy in a single strike. The great "power" and that which causes the enemy to reflect one thousand times are a result of the "powers" of the groups, whether they are groups of "vexation" or groups of administration in the regions of savagery. The tie of religious loyalty between all of these groups is embodied in a covenant written in blood. The most important clause of this covenant is: "Blood for blood and destruction for destruction." We note that we consider our jihad in this stage to be the jihad of an *ummah*. Therefore, the rule of Islam has been firmly established for each individual, group, or band, and they enter the jihad and exchange loyalty with us on the basis of "blood for blood and destruction for destruction." They are a part of the mujahid movement, even if they differ over the correct method in intellectual and operational matters, as long as these differences are over interpretation rather than intent.

Therefore, we must respect those among the sects or among the general public who desire jihad and give their loyalty to us. We accept them, help them, and assist them, without imputing any error to them and trying to correct it, as long as it does not cause *fitnas* [civil war or disagreement within Islam] and harm that might afflict the jihad, especially since its benefit [i.e., tolerating their errors] will usually be greater than the harm that results. There is no doubt that the mutual exchange of loyalty and assistance among the groups has taken place, especially those that follow the High Command. Regrettably, however, when the theater of operations widens and the enemy blunders into igniting a confrontation with the entire *ummah* or among the Islamic movements not previously in opposition, we expect to see the appearance of groups among the masses or among the movements who will not exchange loyalty with the jihadist movement on account of the disunion that exists in the *ummah*. If that stage confronts us, our role—even if we were originally striving to unite the *ummah* under a single banner—is to spread awareness among the classes of people of the *ummah* as to the importance of uniting goals and methods and exchanging loyalty.

An important point remains regarding the subject of achieving the "power," especially regarding how to estimate the force at our disposal and then to build our activities and plans on the basis of sound data. Regarding this point, we wish to emphasize that we must not build our activities based on the support of those whose loyalty we do not command and whom we do not direct.

The Political Game

We urge that most of the leaders of the Islamic movement be military leaders or have the ability to fight in the ranks, at the very least. Likewise, we also urge that those leaders work to master political science just as they would work to master military science. During our long journey through victories and defeats, through the blood, severed limbs, and skulls, some of the movements have disappeared and some have remained. If we meditate on the factor common to the movements that have remained, we find that there is political action in addition to military action. Of course, some of them practiced nonsharia policies in some situations and managed to survive, even though their survival was, naturally, devoid of blessing. However, there are also those in other Islamic movements who understand the politics of the enemy and their fellow travelers and interact with them according to sharia policy. They became an entity that grew through the blessing of acting to assist the religion and the blessing of not violating the sharia. As for the fate of the movements that undertook jihad, battle, and military action and neglected politics and considered it a filthy activity of Satan, or those groups that delved into practicing nonsharia political methods and were engrossed in infidel politics, regrettably their fate was to become a tool for the powers of unbelief and apostasy in order to pluck the fruits of jihad.

Political action is very important and dangerous, such that one of them said: "A single political mistake leads to a result that is worse than one hundred military mistakes." Despite the hyperbole in this statement, it is true to the extent that it clarifies the seriousness of a political mistake. Of course, when some of us witness the decay in the political attitudes of the people and find that they have lost their morals and humanity and are following satanic methods filled with deception, lies, conspiracies, and treason, they are inclined to abstain from engaging in the decay of those politics. However, we should not abandon politics.

Likewise, there are those who engage in disciplined political action—commensurate with their knowledge of it—in addition to military action. Regrettably, however, they still do not understand the reality of the political game of the enemies and their fellow travelers. The interest in understanding the rules of the political game and the political reality of the enemies and their fellow travelers and then mastering disciplined political action through sharia politics and opposing this reality is not less than the importance of military action, especially if we consider that the moment of gathering the fruit—a moment that is considered the recompense for the sacrifices offered by the mujahideen during long decades—is a moment resulting from a political strike and a decisive political decision. Of course, military strikes preceded and even accompanied it, but the final moment and the fate of the movement depends on skillful political management. Even the whole course of fighting requires good political management so that the best results can be achieved. Additionally, there is a very important point: Political management means the political decisions issued by the military leader or the political administration, most of which should be made up of warriors. These are the people who should take an interest in studying the political dimension. The political battle is their battle before it is the battle of others, so one should emphasize the danger of leaving political decisions in the hands of those who do not engage in military battles—for any reason. Here I will briefly set forth a small section on the rules of the political game played by the enemies and their fellow travelers.

- The aim that motivates our enemies is a material aim. Thus the doctrine of conflict that the people of unbelief and apostasy possess is a material, worldly doctrine in most of its structure. If they have worldly motives, they conceal them with religious or false, so-called cultural motives. However, what fuels their actions is material interests and the desire to survive. Thus they strive to survive, but it is not just any survival; rather, it is a survival that guarantees for them an unruffled life of comfort and luxury. As for their allies and those who support them, they continue and remain steadfast in their coalition with them as long as their interest is served by that alliance.

- Thus the most important of their political principles is the principle of self-interest. This principle absolutely does not submit to any moral value; rather, all other principles are subordinate to it—friendship or enmity, peace or war—and are all determined according to self-interest.

- The politicians of the West summarize that in a slogan that says, "There is no eternal enmity in politics and no eternal friendship; rather, there are eternal interests." Therefore, the difference of interests among them is a cause for the bloodiest wars. However, that should not make us forget the reality that the shared enmity toward Islam represents a common ground of action for the different communities of unbelief and apostasy.

- Nevertheless, we can also say that their ideological alliance against Islam is a fragile alliance and limited by a ceiling of material interests that each faction possesses. Therefore, we should formulate our military and political plans after properly understanding and appraising the ceiling of interest that limits the action of each one of our enemies and work to widen the gap of interests between hostile factions.

- We can say that bargaining is a characteristic of the politics of the enemy because the substitute for successful bargains between them is continuous war that might crush all of their interests. Therefore they call politics "the art of the possible."

- As for their persistence in continuing war, that is only when they think that their opponent is weak and it is possible to crush his will. When there is violent resistance that leads to invasions that cost a great deal and are of little use, the factions of the coalition began to withdraw one after another, preferring their own security or delaying the conflict until more suitable circumstances.

- The nature of the enemies' bargain does not have the quality of permanence because it is merely a reflection of the scales of power at a particular moment and those scales are always subject to change. Consequently, there is a breach of political treaties that are naturally unmoral.

- Even respecting the agreed-upon bargain is something that is violated under most conditions as soon as possible if the results of that breach are greater than the results of honoring the pledge. Likewise, making contradictory bargains at the same time with factions that have incompatible interests is commonplace in the political jungle.

These are some of the characteristics and nature of the political situation of the enemies and that which has a direct effect on the conflict between Islam and its enemies. As for their fellow travelers among the other Islamic movements, their politics are based on a mixture of sharia politics and the same political principles of the enemy, especially the principle of self-interest. They distort the texts in order to trick the people into believing that their mixture is from the revealed sharia politics. "The human structure of the enemy is weak with regards to battle. He compensates for that by using gadgets, but it is not possible for him to depend on them for ever. Likewise, the enemy compensates for that by using a deceptive media halo and using media deception during each of his movements and when confronting any action from the mujahideen. Therefore, understanding the media politics of the adversaries and dealing with them is very important in winning the military and political battle. One of the most important things that will assist our media policy is to communicate our media material to its intended audiences. One should note that some of the media committees in previous stages failed in communicating to the intended classes of people, especially that material that targeted a certain class of people.

Much media material was often only communicated to the elite, while several other Islamic movements succeeded in communicating their statements and media materials to every home and civilized class. Therefore this important point should not be ignored, especially since we want to communicate our sharia, military, and political positions to the people clearly and justify them rationally and through the sharia and show that they are in the best interest of the *ummah*. Therefore a group should be formed whose purpose is to communicate what we want to say to the masses and focus their attention on it, even if this requires exposing the group to danger that is comparable to the danger of a military operation. It may even necessitate undertaking a military operation to achieve the objective. For example, we kidnap a hostage and then provoke a large outcry over him and demand that the television reporters and the media networks announce what we want to say in full to the people in exchange for handing over the hostage. In the practical example we set forth here, we will show how we can undertake operations against the economy and how to avoid the enemy's media distortion when the enemy undertakes a media campaign that directs accusations against us, beginning with the accusation that we harm the labor force and including the accusation that we are working to impoverish and weaken Islamic nations economically. Naturally, the apostate rulers will try this tactic as we saw when the Islamic Group in Egypt attacked the two sectors of tourism and banks. Though it was not able to effectively target them, it became very clear that it was also unable to confront the media distortion of its activities, even though it targeted sectors that were filled with forbidden practices. What will be the type of distortion that will happen when an economic interest is targeted, such as oil, which is Islamically permissible and is established in the minds of the people as a source that sustains hundreds of millions of Muslims in the Arab and Islamic world?

If we respond to the problems or questions raised in the preceding paragraph, we would smooth the way for targeting any economic target, to say nothing of petrol. Therefore, what is the suggested way of dealing with the problem?

We know that the Islamic Group failed in confronting the media distortion, which was directed toward it when it attacked tourism and banks, as a result of giving two justifications for undertaking this action: First, that it struck a forbidden target. Second, the form of its political justification for targeting the economy of the enemy. Though these were correct justification they were not clearly communicated to the masses. Of course, people reported that these targets were forbidden; however, the second justification—which is the most important—was only communicated to the elite, or rather to some of them, a fact that made the people fail to understand the exact intention of this group. Therefore, the first step in putting our plan in place should be to focus on justifying the action rationally and through the sharia and to argue that there is a benefit in this world and the next for undertaking the plan. Second, we must communicate this justification clearly to the people and the masses such that any means or attempt to distort our action through the media is cut off. Thus the media dimension in this action is our backside, which we will protect.

As a first step a media group must explain that there is no substitute for oil, but that it is the one commodity that is most devalued in price as compared with other commodities. It is even said that the price of a joke told by an actor on the stage is more expensive than a thousand barrels of oil. This study should include a delimitation of a true price for barrels of oil in accordance with sound economic criteria. It must also have an exposition of the political importance of petroleum and the extent of injustice and pillaging the *ummah* has suffered for decades on account of its devalued price. Afterward, the research must be submitted to a member of the committee who specializes in drafting statements of justification. This member will write a statement that should not include a justification that says that we are striking petroleum sectors because it is sold to infidels. That is a legal question and will expose us to media criticism that will turn our action away from its goal. This statement should include the following elements:

1. A summary—in a few lines—of the study that the economic cadre prepared along with a focus on the extent of the injustice that the *ummah* has experienced on account of the devalued price of oil. It should also explain how wealth that was obtained throughout the decades was not used for building the *ummah* as much as it was used as funds for a handful of the collaborators and agents of the West among the Arab and Islamic regimes. It should tell what the present true value of a barrel of oil should be.

2. Announce to all of the states that obtain petrol from Muslim lands that they must pay the true price recorded in the study and the statement, as well as preserve the right of the Muslims in demanding the difference of the price from all previous years. The statement should also announce that we say to whomever disputes this price that this price is what the Muslims are selling their property for. Whoever does not want to pay this price cannot buy it and that the money that will be paid in exchange for the petrol of the Muslims will not enter, after this day forward, into the treasure houses of the regimes that have been bored through with a hole that goes straight to the banks of Switzerland. Rather, popular committees will oversee it and give it to the needy masses. These popular committees will be composed of people among the merchants of the countries and the notables of the Islamic countries who are trustworthy. The announcement should also include a statement that it has issued from a vanguard of the *ummah*

that refuses to see the *ummah* continue to be crushed and deprived of its will.

3. Give an appropriate period of time for compliance with the statement and the taking of serious steps. Otherwise, the striking of petroleum plants will be carried out, especially pipelines where no humans will suffer from striking them or tankers that the infidels command and work on. Thus, striking plants and factories when there are no workers in them avoids harming Muslims and emphasizes that fact to the public. Regarding the guards, if they are among the regime forces belonging to regimes of the collaboration and apostasy, we will deal with them as if they are traitors to their *ummah* who are not inviolable in our eyes.

4. Properly clarifying for the masses that they are in critical circumstances that compel us to do this and that stopping the petroleum sectors from working will not harm our people at all, God willing. First, most of our income from petrol goes into bank accounts belonging to the collaborationist rulers and their assistants and none of it is paid to the masses, save for sprinkling of ashes in the eye. Second, when selling ceases, the petrol will remain in reserves for us and we can sell it afterward for a price that is many times higher than the present price and the disparity of prices will be eclipsed and increase many times over, repairing any destruction that will come to these factories over a short period of time. Thus we hope that the condition of the *ummah* will change and that it will reclaim its will and its rights and its wealth, which the West and its collaborators among the traitorous rulers have plundered. We do not do this except for the sake of the welfare of the *ummah* and they must reject the campaign of distortions by the regimes that will be unleashed in order to distort our goals and our actions. If we are endowed with but a little patience, the *ummah* will reclaim its standing and its prestige.

The second step: We work to communicate the economic study to as many people as possible among the economic, political, and media elites in the Islamic world and outside of the Islamic world in order to inform them of the extent of injustice that afflicts the poor masses in our *ummah* and also to encourage the petroleum states in non-Islamic regions to raise the price of petrol on their part, even if this requires kidnapping a Crusader manager or engineer—it is preferable that he be an employee in the petroleum sectors—who will not be released until the condition of announcing the statement in the newspapers and the television channels has been completely met. The kidnapping operation can be undertaken, for example, in Nigeria or Senegal or any Islamic petroleum country, even if the planned operations afterward will be undertaken in other places, like the [Persian] Gulf, for example. If kidnapping a Western Crusader is difficult, it is possible to kidnap one of the Arab Christians who work in the petroleum sectors. Likewise, it is possible for the kidnapped person to be a Western reporter and others who are easy to kidnap from among people who are not employees in the petroleum sector, if kidnapping him serves the media plan connected with this operation. Instead of the kidnapping operation, it is possible to undertake any act that will capture the attention of the world and make it want to hear the statement that will follow that action.

It is anticipated that after undertaking the two previous steps there will be no response from the West to our demands. There will also be an attempt to ignore the threat, even though they will approach it with a high degree of seriousness, especially if its announcement has been made by means of a hostage-taking operation. Likewise, it is also anticipated that our limited operations, which will follow the elapse of the specified time mentioned in the statement, will not stop the pumping of petroleum to the West. However, at least these operations will raise the price of oil, even if it is just covering the cost of the electronic security system and the salaries of troops and guards who will be disbursed along the paths of the oil pipelines and the massive factories of the petroleum sectors and their many annexes. We also anticipate an additional increase in the price of petroleum during the political crisis the operations will cause. We also anticipate a rise in the price of petroleum even before the operations take place solely on account of the statement and the study that are issued. Some may be surprised even more if we say that all of the previous is not important and that all of the results we mentioned in the previous paragraph are not important to us, regardless if they are the negative results we have anticipated or a response to the demands that has not been anticipated. Rather, what is important to us is the withdrawal of the elite forces of the enemy in large numbers to economic locations in order to protect them. When the best forces are positioned to protect thousands of petroleum or economic locations in a single country, the peripheries of that country and the crowded regions will be devoid of forces. Even if they are found there, they will be weak forces that will be easy to confront. Therefore, we make no agreements or deals with the troops and officers of the regimes of apostasy. However, we will not kill them if they leave us alone to train, to propagate our message, and to enlist other people freely in crowded regions and in the peripheries of the country. If they oppose us, they will receive only the sword from us. By this means, large steps will be taken toward the stage of the management of savagery and forcing the weak, neglected troops of apostasy who are abandoned in the peripheries and the crowded regions to choose between being killed, joining us, or fleeing and abandoning their weapons.

They will leave the management of the regions to us, which will have begun to suffer from the government's weakness and from the growth of gangs. We must deal with it and manage this savagery.

Likewise, I want to tell those who are concerned about the media distortion and the media campaigns directed against us to relax and prepare yourselves for what is greater than that, or else we will never be fit for a jihad. We must pay no mind to campaigns like these, and we must prepare to ward them off as much as possible. If not now, then when? Inform him who puts his foot on the path of jihad that the day may be upon us when the battles will flare. On that day we will see millions of people emigrating from the regions, fleeing the violence of battle with the regimes of apostasy or the Crusader-Zionist regimes, as happened when the battles flared up in Afghanistan and Chechnya. We will face media campaigns—the brilliant scholars among the leaders of the Islamic movements may even participate in them—since we will be blamed for the refugees. And perhaps we will be blamed for the waves of bombing by the armies of apostasy and the Crusade that kill thousands, and we must prepare ourselves for that, as one of the Afghan leaders did. He was sitting with Sheikh 'Abd Allah 'Azzam when a message came to him informing him of the murder of more than twenty of his family members during the bombing of one of the villages while the man continued talking. The sheikh said to him, "What is the news that came to you?" The man informed him of it. Sheikh 'Abd Allah says, "He tells me how many of his kindred were killed as if he were talking about making the pilgrimage one year." They finished what they were discussing and it was as if nothing had happened. Such is war, and the masses must become accustomed to it. If not now, then when? And how else will we make our way out of the labyrinth? We must prepare, as much as possible, to respond to the campaigns of distortion. If we are sincere in our action and master it, our words will reach the hearts of the people and our staff will smite every falsehood they circulate regarding us. The people will be patient with us as long as we are in the vanguard of those who are patient. But if we begin to complain, lament, and worry, then the people have the right to be worried about us.

I want to reiterate that what we have mentioned here regarding petroleum is only an example for stimulating the mind. However, the strategy of targeting the economy of the enemy in general is a valuable strategy both politically and militarily, and it should not be absent from the guiding movement.

A Blazing Battle ... The Media ... Mastering Management ... Raising the Status of Faith ... Direct Speech ... Forgiveness ... Uniting through Money ...

The most marvelous have been realized through the politics of the renewal movement and we have become unafraid. The consequence is the polarization of the *ummah* has reached its furthest extent. By polarization, I mean dragging the masses into the battle such that polarization is created between all of the people. Thus one group of them will go to the side of the people of truth, another group will go to the side of the people of falsehood, and a third group will remain neutral, awaiting the outcome of the battle in order to join the victor. We must attract the sympathy of this group and make it hope for the victory of the people of faith, especially since this group has a decisive role in the later stages of the present battle. Dragging the masses into the battle requires more actions that will inflame opposition and will make the people enter into the battle, willing or unwilling, such that each individual will go to the side that he supports. We must make this battle very violent, such that death is a heartbeat away, so that the two groups will realize that entering this battle will frequently lead to death. That will be a powerful motive for the individual to choose to fight in the ranks of the people of truth in order to die well, which is better than dying for falsehood and losing both this world and the next. This was the policy of battle for the pioneers: to transform societies into two opposing groups, igniting a violent battle between them whose end is either victory or martyrdom, whose emblem is either glorious war or humiliating peace. One of the two opposing groups is in paradise and the other is in hell: "Our fallen warriors are in Paradise and their fallen warriors are in Hellfire."

This battle alone, through its vehemence and its ability to separate people, is that which will enable us to polarize the largest number of individuals toward our ranks such that we will not grieve afterward over those who are destroyed. We rejoice for him whom God has chosen for martyrdom.

There is no doubt that when the battle escalates, and is set ablaze, hearts and minds will be moved and this violence will furnish the greatest proof to the people. Thus polarization will increase. However, we find that every stage of our battle needs methods that are soft in order to counterbalance that violence so that the situation will be in good order, especially since the classes of people we should focus on polarizing will be different in every stage of the battle. In the stage of "the power of vexation and exhaustion," we need to polarize the elect among the youth of the *ummah*, and the best way to do that is through justifying the operations rationally and through the sharia. The highest degree of justification is to justify the act itself by itself. However, in the face of the hostile media it is difficult to create an operation that justifies itself. When the groups advance and grow and their operations coalesce, they will be able to prevent the media from monitoring them and distorting their goals. As for the stage in which the hostile media is active, there is no way to justify the operations save by issuing published statements. Statements through audio or visual media prepare everyone for the operations before they are undertaken—without specification, naturally—and they are justified afterward through a powerful, rational, sharia-based justification. These statements should be communicated to the people, not just to the elite. Most of the statements should include our general goals that are acceptable to the people, even if they are not stated explicitly: We fight in order to get rid of the enemies of the *ummah* and their agents who have destroyed the beliefs of the countries and plundered their wealth and made us into their servants. As everyone can see, they are clearly destroying everything. They are even extracting the cost of their murder and destruction from us. As for polarization the stage of "the management of savagery," it begins to take on another kind of importance. When savagery happens in several regions, a spontaneous kind of polarization begins to happen among the people who live in the region of chaos. The people, seeking security, rally around the great personages of the country or a party organization or a jihadist organization or a military organization composed of the remainders of the army or the police of the regimes of apostasy. In this situation, the first step of polarizing these groups begins so that they may enter into mutual professions of loyalty with the people of truth by establishing administrative groups that are subordinate to us. Immediately after we assume administration of a region proper media propaganda concerning the situation of our regions with respect to security, justice by means of implementing the sharia, solidarity, preparation, and training must be instituted. We will find that along with this first step there will be a continuous emigration of the youth of other regions to our regions in order to assist them and live in them, despite the loss of lives and worldly gains or the pressure of the enemies upon these regions.

We often find that there are regions that fall under the administration of tribes. On account of their solidarity, their power will increase despite the different hostile powers surrounding them, such as the remainder of the forces of the regimes of apostasy, organized gangs, and the raids of the Crusaders. When we address these tribes we should not appeal to them to abandon their solidarity. Rather, we must polarize them and transform them into praiseworthy tribes. They have power and capacity, so our message should not seek the dissipation of this power—aside from the difficulty of doing so. It is more preferable to change the trajectory of their power so that what it will be set upon the path of God, especially since they are prepared to sacrifice for the sake of the principles and honor they believe in. It is possible to begin doing so by uniting the leaders among them with money and the like. Then, after a period of time in which their followers have mixed with our followers and their hearts have been suffused with the picture of faith, we will find that their followers do not accept anything that contradicts the sharia. Of course, solidarity remains, but it has been changed into a praiseworthy solidarity instead of the sinful solidarity they used to have.

When we begin administering some of the regions, financial revenues will rush in upon us from charitable giving, whose secure arrival in this circumstance can be guaranteed by various means more preferable than the current situation. Likewise, there is money obtained from financial institutions that we will plunder from what the regimes of apostasy leave behind when they depart these regions. Naturally, these institutions will be of the small or medium sort. As for the companies, factories, and massive institutions such as petroleum and the like, the regimes of apostasy will concentrate all of their forces around them in order to protect them, as we mentioned previously.

In the beginning, we stressed that our battle is a battle against unbelief and faith against polytheism and it is not an economic, political, or social battle. However, we must not forget that part of sharia politics is to address those who have weak souls among the different classes of people with the promise of reclaiming our money and our rights, or rather plundering the money of God that evil people have taken. We do not think that a promise like this motivated the companions of the Prophet. Rather, it was a distraction for them and a motivation for the weak souls among the people to accept Islam. Afterward, it is clear that these weak souls improved their condition by living among the people of faith and the furnace of battle, and their motivation was for the sake of Islam before all else.

It remains for the federation of truth composed of our firm bases and the mujahid youth to know the details of the laws for uniting the hearts with money. Among them is the following: One who kills for the sake of money will receive no recompense in the hereafter. One whose intent for money is secondary and whose primary intent is that the word of God be exalted diminishes his recompense in heaven. The rules are as follows:

- One who is sound of body and plunders is paid one third of his share in advance.
- One who sheds his blood and whose property is destroyed takes his recompense fully.

Mastering the Security Dimension: Surveillance and Infiltrating Adversaries and Opponents of Every Kind

Our battle is long and still in its beginning. Its length provides an opportunity for infiltrating the adversaries and their fellow travelers and establishing a strong security apparatus for ourselves. We should infiltrate the police forces, the armies, the different political parties, the newspapers, the Islamic groups, the petroleum companies (as an employee or as an engineer), private security companies, sensitive civil institutions, and so on. This work actually began several decades ago, but we need to increase it in light of recent developments. Likewise, we may need to infiltrate a single place with more than one member—one member will not know another member and vice versa—for different roles or the same role if it requires more than one member.

Several problems will confront us in doing that. Among them is choosing the member who will undertake the infiltration, which must be done with confidence in his ability to safeguard his religion in a field that may be filled with unbelief or things that contradict the sharia. We sometimes have placed a Muslim in the field who is newly pious and thus the problem increases. However, our present and future circumstances bring to light a phenomenon that solves this problem. This phenomenon is the existence of exuberant youth in large numbers seeking jihad, even hastening the undertaking of jihadist operations and martyrdom operations. Their desire for martyrdom indicates a proper condition of faith; all that is required is instructional polishing within the movement. Naturally, most of them will be directed toward jihadist training programs that will take advantage of their abilities and their enthusiasm. However, it is possible to divert some of them to infiltrate the security apparatus and other institutions after it is demonstrated to them recruits that this is important and that it is equal to a martyrdom operation, or that it may even end in a martyrdom operation designed to destroy an infiltrated position. Individual educational programs should also be put in place that teach him to safeguard his piety without revealing it. Frequently, the way of infiltrating and reaching a good position for gathering information requires a long period of time. In that situation, it is possible to give the member freedom of action after giving him a long educational program on the jihad movement, the particular kind of information that is required, how to compile it and preserve it until the time when it is requested from him, or how to communicate it quickly if it is critical information that cannot be delayed.

If the appearance of a region of savagery is delayed, the situation may become difficult for him; for example, continuing his job may affect his piety or he may be on the verge of discovery, and so forth. In this circumstance, he must leave the place of his work and strive to join the mujahideen in the mountains. Or if the situation becomes easy for him, then let him undertake a destructive act against the place where he works to get rid of one or more enemies there. He then withdraws to a secure place until the time he can join the mujahideen.

With regard to individuals who are trusted for their ability to fend off intellectual doubts and bodily desires, infiltrating other Islamic groups and even advancing up their ladder of leadership can lead to many benefits. However, there is the problematic issue of the taboo of spying on Muslims. How is it possible to collect information on them? I believe that this is permissible against movements that harm the mujahideen or interact with the unbelievers. As for infiltrating movements that do not harm the mujahideen, this is not done in order to gather information but, rather, to proselytize among them and to develop a close relationship with them and to benefit from changing their viewpoints regarding what is in the best interests of the jihad in critical circumstances.

The Most Important Problems and Obstacles We Will Face and Ways of Dealing with Them

In this topic, we will deal with the most important problems and obstacles that will confront us. We must only work to solve them without changing the mechanics that guide us according to the principles referred to previously.

The Decreasing Number of True Believers

In the beginning of the Afghani war in the 1970s of the past century, the jihad went through critical periods in which a number of strikes were directed against the mujahideen until—according to some accounts—only thirty men remained. However, after that and after the end of a decade of confrontation with the regime and then in confrontation with the regime and the Russians, the jihad offered up one and a half million martyrs. Where did these numbers of people come from? The answer is that it happened by means of leading the masses to the battle and turning them into an army, especially when we established regions that were secure from the chaos and savagery that resulted from fighting, so that people immigrated to these regions. We can make these regions theaters for proselytizing, training, and education. We will achieve ideal results through using the type of education that is not complete save through battle. Through the atmosphere of battle, they will become ready; nay, they will surpass their teachers.

The Problem of the Lack of Administrative Cadres

The previous problem is connected with another problem, which is our need for a large number of people who have administrative experience, especially in the first periods of the management of savagery. Of course, we have previous experience from managing our organized groups. However, when we settle in the regions, our administrative elements will not be sufficient to manage these regions, whose large numbers of residents will take us by surprise. This situation causes hopelessness and gives birth to doubts, which induce an affection for peace and avoidance of trial. One of the brothers once said to me: "This is not the way that will take us to our goals. Assuming that we get rid of the apostate regimes today, who will take over the ministry of agriculture, trade, economics, etc.?"

The complete answer is that his question and his doubt are based on the notion that the battle is a quick strike, which arises from a deficient understanding of jihad. The leadership will appear during a long journey— a journey of limbs, blood, and corpses. Second, it is not a prerequisite that the mujahid movement has to be prepared for agriculture, trade, and industry. Managers can be paid to run each ministry, who have no interest in policy and are not members of the movement or the party.

More important, there is a better solution for the problem, which is that we get close to the people, perhaps appointing residents of the region that we control to manage some of the jobs with salaries and wages while our men work alongside them without remuneration.

The Problem of Infiltration and Spies

Among the bounties of God to us is that our movement is large and the horrors in which we are immersed reveal for us, one by one, the collaborators in our ranks. Meanwhile, it is possible for the collaborator to live for long years in the ranks of the movements that do not face momentous events, tests, battle, and killing; he may even advance to reach the highest positions within these organizations without anyone discovering him. As for the movements of jihad, show me the collaborator who is willing to participate in a combat operation and expose himself to death. Exposing oneself to death is one of the most important elements for advancement in the guiding movement.

However, the presence of spies may come with the expansion of the movement, especially when we mix with the people in the societies of the regions we manage. However, if we have good relations with the people it is difficult to remove those among them who are spying on us. Rather, the people will be good eyes and armor for us and protect us from spies. Likewise, it is necessary that the punishment for spying and giving loyalty to the enemies of God be harsh in this world and the next. The principles of discovering spies are found in the security reports that the mujahideen usually publish. However, what we want to stress is that the principle of violence, which we mentioned previously, touches on dealing with spies. One who is confirmed as a spy through evidence must be dealt with in a manner that deters others like him. If he flees, he must be followed and not abandoned, even if this takes years. It is necessary to announce that he will receive his punishment, even after long years. This will often make the weak souls hesitate in doing likewise. Likewise, one should issue statements every so often—especially after discovering a spy and punishing him—that the field of repentance is open to whomsoever willingly steps forward to acknowledge that he is under a specific pressure or made a specific error dealing with the enemy. Working to destroy spies with the utmost coarseness and ugliness deters those who merely contemplate undertaking something like spying on us. Media coverage is also important for spreading the cause and justifying it to the people.

The Problem of Excessive Zeal and the Problems That Accompany It, Such as Rushing Operations, Stupidity, or Heresy
As for rushing operations, the prescription for it is understanding and sitting with the youth and clarifying the general policy for action and the importance of biding one's time in some of the stages of the battle in order to drain the enemy. We will show them that this matter will only be mastered by one who is as ponderous as the mountains, who does not easily give in to the provocation of the enemy. Of course, the believer should not be cold emotionally and he should be angry for the sake of God and act to repulse the forbidden things with everything in his power. However, he should know when and how to act so that he can obtain what he desires. Likewise, we should show the youth the importance of listening and obedience, especially regarding matters underlying the wisdom of which we cannot disclose on account of its secrecy. We should also show the importance and seriousness of any action as being part of a more general plan and emphasize the importance of mastering it, even though it may seem small in size and unimportant. This is because the desire for large actions, especially battle, overcomes the minds of some of our enthusiastic people. That is a good quality that usually indicates high aspiration. However, one of its harmful effects is that it moves them to scorn actions that are not large, a fact that may make them listless or make them undertake those smaller actions without mastering them. As for one who insists on haste, it is necessary to remove him from the ranks without cutting the bonds of allegiance. He must be dealt with in a manner that is commensurate with the nature of his problem and his capacity to do other things for the movement. He must be prevented from causing harm to the group by any means allowed by sharia.

Stupidity: As for the zealous person who does stupid things, he must be completely cut off from the ranks, especially in the stage of "the power of vexation and exhaustion" because he may cause a disaster not only for the group that knows him but also for other groups and there may be infinite problems that arise because of him.

Are There Other Solutions That Are Easier Than This Solution?

Some may ask if there are other solutions that are easier than this difficult solution and that spill less blood. Some may also express doubts about this solution and in this important conclusion we will discuss that.

First of all, I want to make an important observation, which is that merely thinking about any corrupt path or baseless doubt is sufficient to expose its corruption without the need for proof, unless the principle is derived from sharia proof.

Some put forward peaceful solutions—such as elections and being limited to peaceful proselytizing—and most people rationally put forward solutions that utilize force by means of a quick, sudden strike that ends everything in a short amount of time without shedding a lot of blood. That strike is carried out in two ways in accordance with the methodology of the one who undertakes it and his mode of thinking. Some advocate a quick strike by means of a military revolt. Others advocate a strike that is undertaken after secret preparations that none know of. They cherish, in everything that they say and plan, the hope of a single strike for which a single preparation may be made, far from the eyes of the adversaries, and by this sudden strike we will destroy the adversaries and avoid much of the blood that is spilled and the spirits that perish. Our sheikhs drone on about this idea frequently, using it as a pretext to gradually move away from the conflict under the slogans of education and preparation. This idea has found an echo and acceptance in the souls because it is very beautiful and very thrilling and very rosy. How can it not be rosy when it comes from the illusions of dreamers? When the dream in one's mind differs with reality, one does not enter into debate with rational and intelligent people.

They dream of a very exalted arrangement for "the power establishing an Islamic state" without passing through "the power of vexation." But this is not possible. It is a deviation and there is no doubt that it is crooked jurisprudence and corrupt law. This jurisprudence that we hear from our sheikhs that permits political diversity and negotiating with those in authority and does not permit offensive jihad and permits appointing infidels to political, military, and judicial positions in the Islamic state only comes about on account of this corrupt dream. The explanation for this is that our world has been filled with evil in all of its dimensions and the Islamic hope has been thwarted.

I found an article by a specialist in political studies in which he censured the movements of jihad for their call to militarize the Islamic movement because the Islamic movement, in his opinion, was entirely a missionary movement. I said: What did the Prophet do with his companions? By my father and mother, did he not militarize them? Who is more learned than him in sharia and universal law? Why should it not be so since God commended him as follows in a *hadith qudsi* [a hadith in which God speaks directly to Muhammad]: "Fight those who disobey you with those who obey you." We know from this that the offensive jihad is the way to freely and effectively spread the call to all of the peoples behind us.

The tyrants plan and plot together for the continued humiliation and pillage of the *ummah*, the suppression of the jihad, and the buying off of the youth and the Islamic movements. Therefore, we must drag everyone into the battle in order to give life to those who deserve to live and destroy those who deserve to be destroyed. We must drag all of the movements, the masses, and the parties to the battle and turn the table over the heads of everyone. We will become a single power by uniting our groups, improving the organization and systematizing the spread of our groups, giving allegiance to each other, assisting each other to the ends of the earth, and by dividing our enemies and their interests. This single force will be able to impose the rule of the sharia and preserve its rights and the rights of humanity, which the unbelievers and apostasy toy with. Thus we must burn the earth under the feet of the tyrants so that it will not be suitable for them to live in, save by professing Islam and being just to the oppressed. Otherwise, they will be destroyed.

Those who follow them are their slaves. They look to the modern civilization of Satan and their sick minds imagine that the awaited nation of Islam is a nation represented in the United Nations, living with its neighbors and having mutual interests with them. The reality is that the Islamic state is predicated on the curtailment of all of that. We, by the grace of God, know sharia and universal laws and hope that God encompasses us with his grace and preserves us through his care until we attain our cherished desires, which is a promise, real and true: "Verily, these are divine promises. If they seemed to be in error to some of us, they will certainly come true for one who stayed firm upon the path and continued the journey. Days and months did not weaken him; rather, he grew firmer and more certain."

CHAPTER 6
The Qur'anic Concept of War

GENERAL S. K. MALIK

The Qur'anic Concept of War *by Brigadier General S. K. Malik of the Pakistani army provides readers with unequaled insight into "proper" Islamic thinking on war. It is by far the best work ever published to match Christian thinking on "just war" doctrine and as such has become a guide within which many radical Islamic groups have tried to fashion their ideology for conflict—with varying degrees of success.*

Malik starts with the presumption that the Qur'an is truly the revealed word of God. This alone makes his theories different from most Christian thinking on war and God. To Muslims, Malik's theories do not express concepts derived by man, but by God. The Qur'an contains God's principles and doctrine of war; hence, one cannot deviate from it. "How to fight wars," for instance, is a "revealed truth" and far above any mere theory. God does not theorize. For Malik, the Qur'anic approach to war is "infinitely supreme and effective."

Originally published in Pakistan in 1979, most available copies are found in India and Pakistan. At present the only translated copy on the Internet has been posted by the U.S. Air Force on their War College site, and though it is sometimes advertised in Muslim bookstores in New York and Washington, D.C., it is usually not available.

Introduction

As a perfect divine document, the Holy Qur'an has given a comprehensive treatment to its concept of war. The Book defines and determines all aspects of the use of "force" in interstate relations. The Qur'anic injunctions cover the causes and object of war, its nature and characteristics, limits and extents, dimensions and restraints. The Book also spells out a unique and distinctive concept of strategy and prescribes its own rules and principles for the conduct of war.

The Qur'anic philosophy of war is infinitely supreme and effective. It strikes a perfect balance between war and policy. It penetrates deep down to systemize and regulate all issues involved in the initiation, planning, conduct, and control of wars. It operates within well-defined divine controls that ensure that war is neither allowed to exceed its scope and purpose nor kept below the optimum level specified. Its laws and principles are universal in nature and abiding in significance. Unlike manmade philosophies, these are neither the product of a given set of circumstances nor made especially for it.

The Holy Qur'an does not interpret war in terms of narrow national interests but points toward the realization of universal peace and justice. It provides an in-built methodology for the attainment of this purpose. This methodology makes maximum allowance to its adversaries to cooperate in a combined search for a just and peaceful order.

This living and dynamic philosophy has, however, suffered from the lack of objective and purposeful research at the hands of both its critics and supporters. The critics misinterpreted it as a form of adventurism, expansionism, and fanaticism. Its supporters concentrated rather excessively on its metaphysical and supernatural aspects but made little effort to highlight its huge scientific and logical approach. This indifference to research, be it willful or inadvertent, has, with the passage of time, prevented us from seeing the Qur'anic military thought in its true light. It has rendered it less assertive, if not altogether extinct, among the rival military concepts and philosophies of the day. A modern military mind, in search of solutions to the complexities of the present-day wars finds little attraction in the study of a philosophy nearly fourteen hundred years old. The gulf between the problems of modern wars and the Qur'anic military thought appears to him to be almost as big and wide as that between an arrow and an atom bomb. As a result, humanity in general and the

Muslim community in particular stand deprived of the unlimited benefits and blessings of this supreme divine philosophy.

There is therefore, an urgent need for updating the research into the subject to find answers to the current and future problems of war. This poses a formidable but by no means insurmountable challenge. To an honest and genuine student of the modern military science, the Qur'anic philosophy of war also presents an equally rich and rewarding field for research. It is, in fact, the crying need of the day. It contains, among numerous other characteristics, a message of hope and assurance for the oppressed peoples of this troubled world.

Divine in conception, the Qur'anic philosophy of war is evolutionary in development and human in application. Within its well-defined parameters, it provides ample scope for human application and research. With all its distinctive import and identity, it is also open to influences from the other philosophies on war and can absorb a great deal of modern military science at the operational level, without sacrificing its own distinctive and fundamental features and principles. To acquire a better understanding and obtain optimum results, we must, therefore, make maximum use of the flexibility that its divine Author graciously provides. But while making conscious efforts to learn from the traditional philosophies on war, we have to resist all temptations of seeking a reflection of our own preferences and inclinations in the Book of God.

A complete and perfect heavenly revelation, the Holy Qur'an is an unlimited reservoir of knowledge, wisdom, science, logic, light, and guidance for mankind till eternity. It has, to use its own words, been revealed as "the Book explaining all things, a Guide, a Mercy, and Glad Tidings to Muslims," and a perpetual and never-ending source of sure and pure inspiration. The Book, as has been admitted by all, is free from all mutilations, modifications, additions, and subtractions. Since its revelation, it is unchanged in its originality, beauty, idiom, diction, phraseology, etymology, science, logic, letter, and spirit. Its accuracy and authenticity is preserved and guaranteed under divine guardianship. "We have," says its divine Author, "without doubt, sent down the message; and we will assuredly guard it from corruption." No other document can match the quality and beauty of the Holy Qur'an.

The divine philosophy on war was not revealed soon after the advent of Islam. It was sent about twelve years later, at a time when nearly two-thirds of the Qur'anic surahs had already been revealed. In marked contrast with the manmade theories and philosophies, the divine concept of war was also not written as a single coherent document, nor administered in one concentrated package or dose; it was, in fact, revealed gradually and progressively. The initial instructions, revealed before the commencement of actual fighting, were brief and sketchy. They dwelt on the fundamental causes of war and spelt out its central theme and object. Also specified in these commands were the controls imposed on the extent, method, and techniques of fighting. Most of the subsequent instructions were revealed in the form of a divine critique on a previous military campaign. These covered, in addition to the specific issues involved in the campaign, the Qur'anic concept of strategy and its principles for the conduct of wars. They also amplified the earlier instructions pertaining to the causes, object, nature, characteristics, dimensions, and ethics of war. Together with their application by the holy Prophet, these divine revelations give a complete and comprehensive coverage to the Qur'anic concept of war.

Historical Perspective

In AD 570, the year of the birth of the Prophet, Abraha, the Abyssinian governor in Yemen, mounted an expedition aimed at destroying the Ka'aba in Mecca but was decisively defeated and destroyed. A reference to this expedition has been made in the Holy Qur'an. "Seest thou not," the Book says, "how thy Lord dealt with the Companions of the Elephant? Did he not make their treacherous plans go astray? And he sent against them Flights of Birds, striking them with stones of baked clay. Then did he make them like an empty field of stalks and straw [of which the corn] has been eaten up."

Meanwhile, the tiny Muslim community in Mecca was the object of the Koraish tyranny and oppression since the proclamation of Islam. They were continuously subjected to the most inhuman torture, repression, and persecution. They were ridiculed, browbeaten, and assaulted; those within the power of the enemy were chained and thrown into prisons; others were subjected to prolonged economic and social tribulations. The enemy repression reached its zenith when the Koraish denied Muslims access to the sacred mosque to fulfill their religious obligations. This sacrilegious act amounted to an open declaration of war upon Islam, and it eventually compelled the Muslims to migrate to Medina, twelve years later, in AD 622.

The Muslim migration to Medina brought in its wake events and decisions of far-reaching significance and consequence for them. While in
Mecca, they had neither been proclaimed an *ummah* nor granted the permission to take recourse to war. In Medina, a divine revelation proclaimed
them an *ummah* and granted them the permission to take up arms against
their oppressors. The permission was soon afterward converted into a
divine command making war a religious obligation for the faithful.

The mission assigned to the new state emphasized its moderation,
balance, practicality, and universality. In subsequent revelations, the Holy
Qur'an ruled, "Ye are the best of Peoples, evolved for mankind, enjoining
what is right, forbidding what is wrong, and believing in Allah." These
proclamations laid the foundations of the political, social, economic, and
military philosophies of the new state and formed the basis of its policy
and strategy. They also set in train a chain of divine revelations pertaining
to state policy and its socioeconomic structure.

Briefly, the newly established state was directed to follow a path of
justice, righteousness, and moderation in all its internal and external
dealings. It was commanded to strike a balance between the extreme
formalism of the mosaic law and the pronounced "other worldliness" of
Christianity. It was also to remain vigilant and ready to act as an arbiter
or a dispenser of justice among the rival systems of the world. In short, as
interpreted by Allama Abdullah Yousaf Ali, it was to live not for itself, but
for mankind.

Concurrent with these declarations, the new state was endowed with
a *qibla* [direction a Muslim should face when praying] in Mecca, replacing
the previously declared one in Jerusalem. The new *qibla* was not only
meant to fix the direction in which the Muslims were to turn in prayers;
it was also to act as a hallmark of their distinctive identity and a symbol
of their international unity.

From its very inception, the microscopic city-state of Medina was
threatened by multiple adversaries. The immediate threat emanated from
the Jewish community of Medina, which had entrenched itself in the city
for the past five hundred years or so. There were also hostile pagan tribes
living around Medina that shared the religious beliefs of the Koraish and
had been having prolonged political and social intercourse with them.
The main threat to the existence of the state, however, came from Mecca,
four hundred miles away, wherein lay the gravitational center of the war
between the Muslims and the pagan Arabia. Yet another adversary, even

more dangerous, that was to jump into the arena soon afterward, comprised the hypocrites. They professed outward loyalties to Islam but were inwardly busy in cutting at its roots.

Among the Persians and Romans a long war continued, but the divine prophecy regarding the defeat of the Persians began to materialize in AD 622 and was to consummate in AD 628. Having assumed control of the Byzantine Empire, Herculius launched a massive and brilliant counteroffensive against the Persians. Passing through the Dardanelles, he crossed into Armenia in AD 623 and conquered Kazwin. The following year, he conquered Cilicia and simultaneously repulsed an attack by the Avers against Constantinople. In AD 627, he defeated the Persians in detail at the battle of Nineveh, forcing their monarch to evacuate Chalcedon, Egypt, and Syria. In AD 628, the Persian king was assassinated and a treaty was signed between the two empires, reestablishing the boundaries of AD 602. Moreover the "True Cross" was handed back to the Byzantines and the divine prophecy stood fulfilled.

A year later, in AD 629, the victorious Roman [Byzantine] armies, returning from Persia, were to measure swords against the Muslims for the first time in the battlefield of Muta. Two years later, they were to concentrate a huge force at Tabuk and pose a direct threat to the security of Muslim Arabia.

After the demise of the Holy Prophet, the Muslims were compelled by circumstances to fight a simultaneous war against the Romans and the Persians. Under the rising sun of Islam, the Persian Empire disappeared from the map of the world by AD 680. By about that time, the Muslims had conquered Syria, Egypt, Anatolia, Cyranica, Tripolatania, and Armenia from the Romans as well.

The Causes of War

Ever since Cain, prompted by feelings of jealousy and hatred, killed his younger brother Abel, human beings have been at war with one another. Research scholars have conducted several studies to identify the causes of these wars. In his scholarly works *The Mathematical Psychology of War and Statistics of Deadly Quarrels*, Lewis. F. Richardson attributed the eruption of wars to a deep-seated disease of the human mind. He further opined that a common cure for war was unfortunately war itself. According to him, severe and intense wars did confer immunity on those who experienced them, but as the next generation appeared, the immunity faded and war was entered upon with renewed enthusiasm. Adam Smith and Thomas Hobbes also concluded that wars were integral to human nature. Arnold Toynbee observed that the human history followed a cycle of war and peace that, on an average, completed its full rotation in a little over one hundred years. In his view, European history completed a full cycle between the period 1815–1914.

Analyzing the causes of the early Muslim wars, historian Quincy Wright attributes them to the harassment and pressure to which Arabia was subjected by her neighbors, the release of surplus energy, economic difficulties, overpopulation, the need to preserve internal unity, the traditional war-mindedness of the Arabs, and the doctrine of jihad. He looks upon the Crusades as the natural outcome of the renewed enthusiasm of Christianity and its recently developed ideology of just wars, political ambition, and economic difficulties.

The current theory is that, wars are caused when vital but incompatible national interests are at stake. "In a sovereign-state system," says Frederick. H. Hartmann, "it can hardly be over-emphasized that war and peace depend upon the decision of each and every state. War is potential in such a system. What converts potential into strife is an incompatibility between the vital interests of two or more states." According to Hartmann, any cause is a significant cause if a state thinks it to be so, and wars occur simply because one sovereign nation decides to invade the other.

In the variety of causes of the war listed so far, a few trends are noticeable. First, these causes suffer from lack of uniformity; different wars have different causes. Second, the causes of war change with the changes and developments in the human society; the tribal society had different causes of war than those prevalent in the present-day international system.

Third, the causes of war cover a wide spectrum, ranging from boredom and frustration to the realization of vital national interests. Fourth, there is no internationally acceptable law, tribunal, or objective criterion to determine the justness of each cause of war. Each nation has its own values and standards for the formulation of its national interests and, consequently, its own causes of war. What can provoke one nation to go to war might not, in the words of Hartman, "ignite even a spark in the other!"

When the Holy Qur'an commanded the Muslims to go to war with their adversaries, it dwelt at length at the causes that necessitated that decision. To understand these causes, we shall, first of all, make an attempt to follow the basic Qur'anic law about the sacredness and preservation of human life.

It will be recalled that when Islam appeared on the scene of the world, human life held little value. In Arabia, Rome, Persia, and in other parts of the world, human beings were killed, burnt or buried alive, and slaughtered like animals or tortured to death for the sake of fun, sport, pleasure, custom, tradition, and superstition. Such merciless killings were resorted to without any fear of accountability before law. Islam rose to denounce these inhuman practices, declared human life sacred and issued strict commands for its respect, preservation, and protection. It prohibited the taking of human life except for reasons of law and justice, and made all unlawful deaths accountable and punishable both in this world and in the hereafter. In the perspective of the Holy Qur'an, such an accountability ensured the preservation of human life and was in the larger interest of the human race itself.

As in the case of individuals, so in inter-state relationship, war could only be waged for the sake of justice, truth, law, and preservation of human society. The central theme behind the causes of wars, as spelt out by the Holy Qur'an, was the cause of Allah. This cause manifested itself in different shapes and forms at different stages in the history of Islam. In the pursuit of this cause, the Muslims were first granted the permission to fight but were later commanded to fight in the way of God as a matter of religious obligation and duty.

The first Qur'anic revelation on the subject that granted Muslims the permission to fight read,

> To those against whom war is made, permission is given to fight because they are wronged; and verily, Allah is most Powerful for their aid. They are those who have been expelled from their homes in defiance of right, for no cause except that they say, "Our Lord is Allah."

A few months after the grant of the permission to fight in self-defense came the divine command making war a religious compulsion and obligation.

> "Fight in the cause of Allah," it said, "those who fight you but do not transgress limits; for Allah loveth not transgressors."

This revelation introduced new elements to the permissible causes of war. Fighting was to be in the cause of Allah. It was to be undertaken only against those who fought Muslims first. During the conduct of war, the limits specified by God were not to be transgressed; those who did so were to incur divine displeasure. Elucidating these points, the Book added:

> And slay them wherever ye catch them, and turn them out from where they have turned you out; for tumult and oppression are worse than slaughter. But fight them not at the Sacred Mosque, unless they first fight you there: but if they fight you, slay them. Such is the reward of those who suppress faith.

The central idea in the divine approach to this issue was that the pagans had no justification to stop the Muslims from performing their religious obligations at the sacred mosque while the latter did not interfere with the rites and rituals of the former.

The Book emphasized the need for fighting in the cause of Allah at several occasions and in various manners and forms: "Then fight in the cause of Allah, and know that Allah heareth and knoweth all things."

Distinguishing the faithful from the unbelievers, the Holy Qur'an observed,

> Those who believe fight in the cause of Allah, and those who reject faith fight in the cause of Evil, so fight ye against the friends of Satan: feeble indeed is the cunning of Satan.

The successful migration of the Muslims from Mecca to Medina was a rude shock to Koraish hopes of destroying Islam. Consequently, they switched their tyranny and oppression over to the recently converted Muslims living in scattered dwellings in the desert.

At the signing of the Treaty of Hudaibiyya, a ten-year peace between Muslims and Meccans was agreed. But the Koraish violated their obligations under the treaty and hatched underhanded plots to discredit the Prophet and to have him expelled from Medina as well. The Book inquired of the Muslims,

> Will ye not fight people who violated their oaths, plotted to expel the Apostle, and took the aggressive by being the first to assault you? Do ye fear them? Nay, it is Allah Whom ye should more justly fear, if ye believe.

It follows, therefore, that the principal cause of war made permissible by the Book was the cause of God. From the human point of view, it was a call for the deliverance of the weak, the ill treated, and the persecuted from the forces of tyranny and oppression. It was the cause of the humanity in general and not that of the Muslim community in particular. Saving the places of worship, irrespective of religious discrimination, and protecting mankind from mischief and bloodshed were causes with a truly universal and humanitarian significance and application. There was no semblance of any kind of adventurism, militarism, fanaticism, national interests, personal motives and economic compulsion in the whole affair. The Book also furnished mankind with an objective criterion of universal validity and application to assess the justness of their causes of war. War was made permissible only to fight the forces of tyranny and oppression.

Interpreting the Qur'anic causes of war for their application to the present-day international system, Dr. Hamid Ullah, in his scholarly work, *The Muslim Conduct of State*, identified a set of circumstances under which an Islamic state could initiate a war with her adversaries. In his opinion, war could be entered upon if the enemy physically invaded the Muslim territory or behaved in an unbearable and provocative manner short of actual invasion. War could also be waged for punitive, retaliatory, and preventive purposes. Permissible also would be to resume a war stopped temporarily for reasons short of a "modus vivendi" or durable peace. A Muslim state could also enter into armed hostilities in sympathy with their brethren living in another state, but only after scrutinizing each case on its own merit and not as a matter of general rule.

The Object of War

When Clausewitz, the founding father of modern military thought, defined war as a "continuation of policy by other means," he threw a challenge to the students of political science and international relations to develop a theory around "policy." Clausewitz thus put the cart before the horse and forced the policymakers to conduct deeper research into the science of politics. It was not "policy" that took the initiative to define the meaning, sphere, limits, and extents of "war." On the contrary, "war" forced "policy" to define and determine its own parameters. It took the human mind hundreds of years to establish, if at all, the relationship between national aims and objectives, national interests, national policy, and war, and even longer to realize that war was subservient to policy. Nonetheless, the political scientists did rise to the occasion to theorize; they opined that, in brief, policy was the pursuit of national interests and that war became an instrument of policy when vital but incompatible national interests were at stake. What they failed to establish, however, was the rationale behind the determination of national interests.

"National interests," concedes Bernard Brodie, "are not fixed by nature nor are identifiable by any generally acceptable standard of objective criteria. They are, instead, the product of fallible human judgment on matters on which agreement within the nation is usually less than universal." That being so, the logical outcome of the concept of national interests in the international system of today is tension and war, and not peace, harmony, justice, and understanding. Indeed, national interests are in a vicious and never-ending cycle of war.

Opposed to the philosophy of national interests, we have a parallel school of thought that advocates that war must result in a durable and lasting peace. Theorists belonging to this school are idealists and have no methodology to offer to implement their thesis. "The object of war," observes Liddell Hart, "is a better state of peace, if only from your point of view." In propounding this theory, Liddell Hart appears to have overlooked the simple rule that peace is essentially a two-sided affair. It is unthinkable that there could be peace without some kind of understanding or accommodation among all the contending parties. Instead of bringing peace and security to mankind, the one-sided peace, imposed upon Germany after the First World War, resulted in greater bloodshed and misery barely twenty years later.

The Yalta Conference, which concluded the Second World War and formulated the Allied postwar strategy, also came under heavy criticism for its inadequacy and shortsightedness. Like other students of politics and war, General Fuller was also its vehement critic. His contention was that the Allied leaders had sacrificed the vital necessity of obtaining a durable peace at the altar of securing the unconditional surrender of Germany. However, this great military thinker had no alternative of his own to suggest to them. As the Second World War came to a close, the Allied war effort also began to give way to their respective national interests. Each side, however, had its own interpretation of what constituted its enlightened national interests. Russia saw her interests in conquering the heart of Europe; the Allies, in the destruction of the German military might.

Considerations of peace weighed heavy on the minds of European nations when they developed the means to destroy one another. Such an atmosphere prevailed after the conclusion of each devastating war and after the atomic explosions of Hiroshima and Nagasaki. But it did not last long. The Europeans soon came to realize that there existed means of protection against weapons that were once looked upon as total and absolute. Once that happened, their baser and destructive elements again overtook the saner ones.

Similar motives underline the present age of "detente" and "deterrence." The considerations of peace come to human mind only when the choice is between "suicide" and "coexistence." They are the by-products of exigency, not of a recognized or consistent policy or philosophy. They failed to stand the test of the time in the past, nor are they resulting in durable global peace at present. Indeed, they have no worthwhile role to play even in the future. The Holy Qur'an spelt out the object of the divine war against paganism soon after it commanded the Muslims to take recourse to fighting. "And fight them on," ruled the Book, "until there is no more tumult or oppression, and there prevail justice and faith in Allah." Similar instructions were repeated after the termination of the Battle of Badr, about a year later. "And fight them on," the Holy Qur'an directed on that occasion, "until there is no more tumult or oppression, and there prevail justice and faith in Allah altogether and everywhere." These injunctions laid down the ultimate and absolute divine purpose behind this war, which was "to obtain conditions of peace, justice, and faith." As discussed previously, the creation of such conditions demanded the eradication of tyranny and persecution. In turn, the eradication of tumult and oppression had several facets, but in essence it meant the restoration of Muslim right of worship in the sacred mosque.

In the initial stages of the attainment of this object, the Holy Qur'an made liberal allowance and concessions to the pagans to cooperate and contribute toward creating just and peaceful conditions. During this period, a number of checks and controls were imposed on the believers to force them to seize the first opportunity to terminate the state of war. They were commanded to reciprocate every move made by their adversaries toward ceasing hostilities or entering into peace with them.

> "But if they cease," the Book directed them, "let there be no hostility except to those who practice oppression."

This implied that, in such a situation, there was to be no rancor against the enemy. The Muslims were to follow the "oft-forgiving and most-merciful" nature of their Lord and forgive their foes. Likewise, the Book commanded the believers, "But if the enemy inclines toward peace, do thou also incline toward peace, and trust in Allah: for he is the One that heareth and knoweth (all things). Should they intend to deceive thee, verily Allah sufficient thee."

The divine emphasis on reciprocating the enemy inclination toward peace raised the question of entering into treaties and alliances with them for which a clear-cut philosophy and methodology had to be prescribed. On this issue, the Holy Qur'an gave the Muslims a theory based on justice, equality, and reciprocity. It was a theory that applied equally to the covenant between man and God, and the treaties and alliances between nations and states.

The Book warned those who, having entered into a covenant with their Lord, broke it and embarked upon disruption and mischief. Said the Holy Qur'an:

> Those who break Allah's Covenant after it is ratified, and who sunder what Allah has ordered to be joined, and do mischief on earth: these cause losses only to themselves.

As in the case of the covenant between man and God, so in interstate agreements, the observance of a treaty was a two-way traffic. The Muslims could not go on fulfilling their part of the agreement if the pagans kept violating theirs. They could honor their commitments only if the latter also did likewise.

What about those pagans who violated the principle of reciprocity and broke their treaties? The Books said that should Muslims suspect treachery from the pagans they are permitted to revoke their treaties.

The above policy remained in force for a period of nearly eight years, that is, from AD 622 to 629. During this period, some pagan tribes did remain true to their treaties with the Muslims. A majority of them, however, entered into agreement to seek a timely escape from a difficult situation and renounced it each time they could gain an advantage over Muslims or cause them some damage. After such a prolonged tolerance, the Almighty Lord eventually decided to issue his commands to deal with this dissident and treacherous group. It was decided to bear no further responsibility to the treaties concluded with them and revoke them altogether. A formal announcement to this effect was made to the Arabian tribes gathered in Mecca for the pilgrimage, a few months later.

To those pagans with whom the treaties were abrogated, a grace period of four months was allowed to reshape their strategy and begin to honor their treaties. Should they fail to avail themselves of this facility, the Holy Qur'an directed the Muslims to "fight and slay the Pagans wherever ye find them." The Almighty Lord, however, gave a chance to those who faithfully observed their pledge, to continue their alliance till the end of its term. These revelations commanded the Muslims to fulfill their treaty commitments for the contracted period but put them under no obligations to renew them.

In the final stage, all those living in Arabia who did not embrace Islam, including the Christians and the Jews, were given the option to choose between "war and submission." As a token of their willing submission, they were called upon to pay the *jizya* to the Islamic state. The root meaning of *jizya* is "compensation." In its technical sense, it was a tax levied on those who did not embrace Islam but were willing to live under the protection of the Islamic state and enjoy personal liberty of conscience. As interpreted by Allama Abdullah Yousaf Ali, the *jizya* was partly symbolic and partly a commutation for military service, being a tax on able-bodied males only. Ruled the Holy Qur'an:

> Fight those who believe not in Allah nor The Last Day, nor hold that forbidden which hath been forbidden by Allah and his Apostle, nor acknowledge the Religion of Truth, (even if they are) of the People of the Book, until they pay the *jizya* with willing submission, and feel themselves subdued.

The divine instructions on the object of war also covered the Muslim policy toward the "hidden" enemies, that is, the hypocrites. The Holy Qur'an warned Muslims about the intentions of the hypocrites, saying:

> They but wish that ye should reject Faith, as they do, and thus be on the same-footing as they.

As to the policy to be adopted toward them, the Book suggested two alternative courses of action. First, it advised the believers not to take friends from their ranks until they submit themselves to discipline. Second, should they turn renegades, the Book directed the faithful to:

> Seize them and slay them wherever ye find them.

These instructions provide us the basis for adopting a suitable policy and strategy toward the hidden enemy of today that manifests itself in the form of antistate elements, enemy agents, saboteurs, propagandists, and partisans. Should they persist in their evil designs, they are to be treated at par with the known or the declared enemy.

To recapitulate, in the Qur'anic perspective, the object of war is to obtain conditions of peace, justice, and faith. To do so, it is essential to destroy the forces of oppression and persecution. In the initial stages of its realization, the Holy Qur'an made generous concessions to the adversaries to terminate the state of war and invited them to contribute in creating conditions of harmony and peace. The law of equality and reciprocity was observed in dealing with treaties and alliances. But as the enemy went on rejecting one divine concession after another, it became necessary to adopt a harder line. A declaration of immunity from the treaty obligations was pronounced to those who played treacherously with the Muslims, but strict commands were issued to fulfill the treaty obligations with those who remained loyal and true. The doors of compassion, forgiveness, and mercy were always kept open, and those offering genuine repentance were forgiven. In the final stages, the pagans were forbidden from performing their rituals in the sacred mosque, and those who did not embrace Islam were called upon to either pay the *jizya* as a token of their willing submission or accept war. Those who paid the *jizya* were given freedom of religion and the protection of the Muslim state.

The Nature and Dimensions of War

In the traditional thinking, the nature and pattern of war is said to be in a constant state of change and evolution. At various stages of the development and evolution of the philosophy of war, military thinkers propounded different theories about the nature, pattern, dimensions, and characteristics of war. Until about the eighteenth century, students of war were familiar with its physical dimensions only. During the past two centuries, however, both military theorists and its renowned practitioners had begun to identify the moral and psychological forces involved in the planning and conduct of war. As time passed, these factors assumed greater importance, until psychological factor came to be considered as the decisive factor. The physical dimensions of war were relegated to a position of secondary importance and found to be meaningless without moral and psychological backing.

In the European military history, Napoleon was among the pioneers to stress and demonstrate the ascendancy of psychological factors in war. The crusade was kept up by Liddell Hart, who considered it as the all-important and most-decisive element of war. An ardent critic of Clausewitz in several other fields, Liddell Hart acknowledged Clausewitz's contribution in introducing moral factors to warfare. Psychological warfare has since become a recognized, indeed, specialized, branch of war.

Scores of other studies have been conducted into the subject. In his book, *The Art of War on Land*, Colonel Burns identified a set of four strands that, in his opinion, combined together to win a war. Burn's strands, to which he did not attach any relative weights, were the commander, the troops, morale, and resources. The commander's strength was to be determined by his personality, knowledge, and capacity for planning; that of the troops by their training and technical efficiency. Morale included everything that conferred upon the troops the will to win the war, while resources comprised the numbers, armaments, supplies, and transport. Burns compared these strands with the fibers of a cord and ruled that the strength of the cord was to be determined by the total strength of all the fibers. An army might be relatively weak in one strand but could be strong in the aggregate. In the winning of wars, it was the total strength of the "cord" that mattered and not that of the individual strand.

With evolution in the subjects of science, technology, and international relations, corresponding changes have come in the theories and concepts about the nature and dimensions of war. Concepts like the national wars, nation-at-arms, ideological wars, economic wars, limited wars, and total and general wars are the product of these developments. Not long ago, warfare was looked upon as the exclusive province of the soldier. Today it is regarded as a multidisciplinary function that demands the application of all the elements of national power. Indeed, it is considered to be too serious a business to be left to the soldier alone.

The dimensions given to war by the Holy Qur'an take into account the divine purpose behind the creation of man and guide him to his ultimate destiny. In determining them, the Book has penetrated deep down to identify and unfold the "real" issues involved in the planning and conduct of wars. The fountainhead of these dimensions lies in the fact that the cause of war is the cause of Allah. To proceed from this base, the Book commands Muslims to wage their war with the spirit of a religious duty and obligation.

> Fighting is prescribed for you, and ye dislike it but it is possible that ye dislike a thing which *is* good for you and that ye love a thing which is bad for you.

This Qur'anic injunction adds new facets and depths to the concept of a total war. It makes a Muslim citizen answerable both to the state and to Allah in the fulfillment of this divine obligation. When prescribed, it also looks upon war as something virtuous for the faithful and beneficial for the rest of the humanity. The biggest virtue of this war lies in its cause and object. A war fought to end repression and to create conditions of justice and peace cannot but be noble and virtuous.

Upon the foundations furnished by this master dimension of war, the Book proceeds to raise a grand edifice. To those who fight for the cause of Allah, the Holy Qur'an made promises of generous heavenly assistance.

> "O ye who believe I," it said, "if ye will aid the cause of Allah, he will aid you, and plant your feet firmly."

It left them in no doubt about the impact and import of the divine aid. "If Allah helps you, none can overcome you," the Book claimed. On the other hand, the Book emphasized that none would come to the help and assistance of those who rejected the faith.

The Holy Qur'an then goes on to spell out the traits and qualities of the people who deserve God's aid. It demands Man's total submission as the "price" of heavenly help. Elaborating further, the Book rules that God's blessings are meant for those men of faith and devotion, who, when afflicted with calamity, say,

> To Allah we belong, and to him is our return.

At a subsequent occasion, the Creator of the Universe enters into a bargain with the faithful.

> Allah hath purchased of the Believers, their persons and their goods; for them in return is the Garden of Paradise.

They fight in his cause, and slay and are slain: a promise binding on him in truth, through the law, the gospel, and the Qur'an—and who is more faithful to his covenant than Allah? Then rejoice in the bargain which ye have concluded: that is the achievement supreme.

The Book, however, made it clear to the believers that heavenly assistance promised to them was not a matter of right or routine. They had to come up to the divine standards and qualifications to earn the divine aid. Should they fail to do so, they would not only forsake the divine help but would also run the risk of incurring Godly wrath.

The divine verdict on the question of heavenly help to the believers while fighting against their adversaries thus stands clear and undisputed. God has not reserved his bountiful blessings for any community of people as such. Muslims would be making a grave mistake if they took his help for granted, without first qualifying themselves to obtain it. God does not change the condition of a people who do not first effect a change inside their own hearts and souls. He helps only those who help themselves; and bestows this honor only upon those who genuinely deserve it.

Prior to Islam, the Israelis mistook themselves as God's chosen people and came to grief, but their progeny have since learned their lesson and are no longer repeating that mistake. Let us, therefore, be in no doubt that we are entitled to only that which we earn and strive for. We cannot harvest any more than what we grow and nourish. Should we fail to come up to the divine standards, we shall not only lose heavenly help and assistance but might incur God's wrath instead.

Fighting causes danger to life and property; it results in hunger, thirst, fatigue, injury, death, destruction, and devastation. The Holy Qur'an acknowledged these horrors of war and dealt with them in a logical and scientific manner. In this regard, the Book gave mankind a distinctive philosophy of life, death, reward, and punishment. According to the Book's injunctions, death in this world, no doubt, inevitable, was nevertheless not to be the end of life. Another life awaits us in the hereafter. Against this perspective, the Book called upon the faithful to fight in the way of Allah with total devotion and never contemplate flight from the battlefield or fear death.

Having spelt out the divine verdict on the inevitability of death and on life after death, the Book gave its ruling on those who die fighting for the cause of God:

And if ye are slain, or die, in the way of Allah, forgiveness and mercy from Allah are far better than all they could amass. Think not of those who are slain in Allah's way as dead. Nay, they live, finding their sustenance in the Presence of their Lord. They rejoice in the Bounty provided by Allah.

The divine reward was to vary according to the performance of the believers. Said the Book:

> Not equal are those believers who sit at home and receive no hurt, Allah hath granted a grade higher to those who strive and fight with their goods and persons than to those who sit at home.

On the other hand, the Book warned those who hated to strive and fight in the cause of Allah, who rejoiced themselves in their inaction, and who wanted to save their skins from the hazards of the battle that "the fire of Hell is fiercer in heat if only they could understand!"

To recapitulate, the fountainhead of the Qur'anic dimensions of war lies in the fact that war is waged for the cause of Allah with the object of imposing conditions of justice and peace. To those who fight for this noblest heavenly cause, the Book promises handsome heavenly assistance. The index of fighting for Allah's cause is man's total submission to his will. Those who fail to submit themselves fully and completely to the will of God run the risk of incurring heavenly wrath. Fighting involves risk to life and property that must be accepted willingly and cheerfully. Death in this world is inevitable, life in the hereafter is certain, and the reward of those who fight for the cause of Allah is safe, splendid, and sure. Our reward is in direct proportion to our performance. Those who die fighting for the cause of Allah never actually die.

For those who believed and practiced them, the Qur'anic dimensions revolutionized warfare in its real sense. They conferred upon them a personality so strong and overbearing as to prove themselves equal to, indeed, dominate, every contingency in war. They dwarfed the psychological and moral dimensions discovered by the human mind. They conferred upon the Muslim armies a complete and total protection and immunity against all the psychological and moral attacks that the enemy could bring to bear upon them. In turn, they provided them with a firm and durable platform to launch effective psychological and moral attacks against their mortal foes. They enabled Muslims to bear the pains of war willingly and resolutely. Knowledge and skills of war followed in the wake of such devoted and spirited men. Learnt and applied with devotion, they proved to be vastly more superior and effective than the "hollow" expertise of the enemies. They helped Muslims conquer the fear of death, and become immortal and invincible.

"Writers on strategy, and certainly its practitioners," says Bernard Brodie, "have almost always rejected from their conscious concern those characteristics of war that to ordinary folk are its most conspicuous ones. In treatises on strategy, battlefields rarely have the smell of death; weapons produce firepower, but no searing din and uproar; men in battle and on the march feel triumph, and sometimes panic, but rarely described are the suffering of pain, cold, sweat, exhaustion, or utter misery." The Qur'anic philosophy of war provides answers to such questions that are bound to agitate the human mind. It recognizes the physical and psychological strains of warfare and provides an effective antidote to them. Given the element of faith and belief in its theories, it pays back exceedingly more than what little we give to it.

The Ethics of War

The Qur'anic philosophy of war is a philosophy of checks and restraints on the use of "force" in interstate relations. The very Qur'anic command that directed the Muslims to go to war with the pagans also bade them not to exceed limits.

> Fight in the cause of Allah, those who fight you, but do not transgress limits; for Allah loved not transgressors.

Divine controls on war were imposed at all stages of the revelation of the Qur'anic message. For the first twelve years Muslims were called upon to put up with the atrocities the Koraish perpetrated on them, to hold back their hands from fighting. With the issuance of the divine command for fighting were also specified the causes for which war could be entered upon. The Holy Qur'an also spelt out a clear and unmistakable object of war. In the initial stages of the attainment of this object, liberal concessions were made to the enemy to terminate war and create conditions of peace. Against all the prevalent norms and practices, no one was allowed to take any life except for reasons of justice and law; those who did not obey this command were made accountable and punished. Finally, the doors of compassion, forgiveness, and mercy were always kept open to those who offered genuine repentance.

The Book commanded Muslims to respect the Arab custom of observing a truce at the sacred mosque, on a reciprocal basis.

> But fight them not at the Sacred Mosque, unless they (first) fight you there.

This was the Qur'anic injunction in the matter. The Qur'anic injunction that "Allah is with those who restrain themselves" speaks of the importance attached to tolerance and forbearance.

Not content with these restrictions alone, the Book imposed a total ban on the inhuman methods of warfare practiced in Arabia and elsewhere, prior to Islam. Based on the instructions issued on the subject by the Prophet and by the Early Caliphs, Muslim jurists have conducted several studies to identify the acts forbidden to the Muslim armies during the fighting. According to Dr. Hamid Ullah, all cruel and torturous ways of killing the enemy are prohibited. The killing of women, minors, servants, and slaves who might accompany their masters in war but do not take part in the actual fighting, is also not allowed. The Muslim armies must also spare the blind, the monks, the hermits, the old, the physically deformed and insane, or the mentally deficient. Forbidden also is the decapacitation of the prisoners of war, the mutilation of men and beasts, treachery and perfidy, devastation and destruction of harvests, excesses and wickedness, and adultery and fornication with captive women. The killing of enemy hostages, and resorting to massacre to vanquish an enemy, is prohibited. The killing of parents except in absolute self-defense, and the killing of those peasants, traders, merchants, contractors, and the like who do not take part in actual fighting, is also not allowed.

A clear and definite divine directive was issued about the prisoners of war.

> Therefore, when ye meet the Unbelievers smite at their necks; at length, when ye have thoroughly subdued them, bind a bond firmly on them: thereafter is the time for either generosity or ransom.

According to this directive, the Muslims were told that, first, their primary consideration in war was to subdue the enemy and not to take prisoners. Second, prisoners could be taken only after the enemy had been thoroughly subdued. Third, once taken, they must be treated humanely; the choice being only between "generosity and ransom."

Revealed as early as the seventh century AD, the Qur'anic checks and controls on war reinforce its claim that war has but a limited and restricted purpose to perform in its overall policy and strategy. They also ensure that, once unleashed, the military instrument does not become uncontrollable. No other philosophy can match the Qur'anic instructions about the humanitarian problem involved in war. They stand guard on the ideology against the irresponsible and malicious criticism leveled against it by its critics. The general pardon proclaimed by the Prophet on his triumphal entry back to Mecca as the unquestioned religious and temporal ruler of Arabia is a shining example of the characteristic Qur'anic restraint in matters pertaining to war. Viewed against the atrocities and bloodshed caused by the world's great conquerors, with which the pages of human history are still reeking, the Qur'anic concept of war is supreme both in its humanitarian and moral contents.

A common charge leveled by the critics against Islam is that it has spread through the sword; a charge that most of its supporters vehemently refute. The truth is that the checks and controls imposed by the Holy Qur'an on the use of force have no parallel. In practice, there were but few isolated instances where the Muslims transgressed these limits, but the Prophet disapproved of them. It must, however, be understood that the exercise of restraint in war is essentially a two-sided affair. It cannot happen that one side goes on exercising restraint while the other keeps on committing excesses. In such a situation, a time comes when the very injunction of preserving and promoting peace and justice demands the use of limited force. It would be sinful to withhold the use of force under those circumstances. Islam permits the use of the "sword" for such a purpose. Rather than be apologetic about it, a Muslim should be proud of the fact that, when used, his sword is meant to subdue the forces of tyranny and repression, and to bring peace and justice to mankind. And it is withheld the very moment these conditions are obtained.

In Islam, a war is fought for the cause of Allah. A Muslim's cause of war is just, noble, righteous, and humanitarian. A victory in Islam is a victory for the cause of Islam. So noble and humanitarian a cause cannot be allowed to be attained through inhuman and undignified ways. Humanitarianism thus lies at the very heart of the Islamic approach to war.

The Strategy for War

Before studying the Qur'anic concept of strategy, it is essential to carry out a selective analysis of its evolution so as to acquire an idea of the stages through which human thought has passed on this subject. In an article pertaining to the evolution of strategic thought, Harry L. Coles expresses the view that the history of strategy can be divided into two time groups: the pre-1945 time group, during which strategy suffered from under think, and the post-1945 period in which it has been suffering from the opposite malady—the overthink. The climax of the pre-1945 strategic thought was the discovery that the decision should be sought in the psychological dimensions of war. With the advent of the nuclear bomb in the post-1945 period, the theory of strategy has, after passing through several evolutionary stages, eventually come to be dominated by "deterrence."

In the early nineteenth century, Clausewitz defined strategy as "the art of the employment of battle to gain the object of war," a concept to which Moltke, Schlieffen, Foch, and Ludendroff also religiously subscribed. The crux of their thesis was that, in war all other considerations should be subordinated to the main consideration of fighting a decisive battle. A century later, Liddell Hart rose to denounce Clausewitz on two scores. His first objection was that Clausewitz's strategy intruded into the sphere of policy. The second note of discord was that it confined the means of strategy to the pure and exclusive utilization of battle.

Opposed to the "blood-red wine of Clausewitzian growth," Liddell Hart courted the idea of "bloodless victories" and termed it as "perfect strategy." As examples of perfect strategy, he cited Caesar's Illerda campaign, Cromwell's Priston campaign, Napoleon's Ulm campaign, Moltke at Sedan in 1870, Allenby's Samaria campaign in 1918, and the German conquest of France in 1940. In Liddell Hart's language, strategy was "the art of distributing and applying military means to gain the ends of policy." The aim of strategy, he contended, was to produce a strategic situation so advantageous that "it does not of itself produce the decision, its continuation by battle is sure to achieve this." Psychological dislocation of the enemy directed at producing a direct decision was thus the primary aim of Liddell Hart's strategy. "If this was not possible," he conceded, "then a physical or logistical dislocation must precede battle, to reduce fighting to the slenderest proportion."

It follows that dislocation, the central theme of Liddell Hart's strategy, could be produced either in the physical or logistical sphere, or in the psychological sphere. Developing his thesis further, Liddell Hart tells us that, in the physical field, dislocation could be caused by upsetting the enemy's dispositions, dislocating the distribution and organization of his forces, endangering his rear and cutting his lines of communication. In the psychological sphere, it was the natural outcome of the physical effects produced on the enemy.

Andre Beaufre, the famed French strategist, agreed with Liddell Hart's theory of the psychological dislocation of the enemy but disagreed with his definition. In Beaufre's opinion, Liddell Hart's definition "hardly differed from that of Clausewitz." Beaufre looked upon strategy as "the abstract interplay of forces which spring from clash between two opposing wills." "In this dialectic of wills," he claimed, "a decision is obtained when a certain psychological effect has been produced on the enemy." The guiding principle in the dialectic of opposing wills was to obtain the decision by creating, and then exploiting, a situation resulting in "sufficient moral disintegration of the enemy to cause him to accept the condition that was desired to be imposed upon him." Lenin, the revolutionary, had earlier laid similar emphasis on the moral factor, though in a different context, by ruling that "the soundest strategy in war was to postpone operations until the moral disintegration of the enemy rendered a mortal blow easy and possible."

Admiral Eccles thought that a correct understanding of strategy was essential since it lay at the very heart of the military problem. He launched a crusade to find harmony and cohesion of concept rather than diversity of ideas and language available in the literature of strategy. He found this identity in the views of Liddell Hart (which we have already studied above) and Herbert Rosinki. Rosinki called strategy "the comprehensive direction of power" and went on to add that the application of strategy was not a mere direction but one that took into account possible counteractions as well. It thus became a means of control, which, in Rosinki's opinion, was its real essence. To Rosinki's definition, Eccles himself proposed an addition. "Strategy," he ruled, "was the art of comprehensive direction of power to control situations and areas to attain objectives." It was essentially concerned with control for a given effect. Elaborating upon the nature of control, he observed, that strategy was concerned with what to control; the purpose, nature, and degree of control; and the method or scheme of control. Like Beaufre, Eccles also recognized that force was only one of the means by which control could be established.

With the invention of the atomic weapons, there appeared, between 1945 and 1955, a class of strategists who looked upon the nuclear bomb as the "absolute" weapon of war. Accordingly, they formulated the balance of terror theory, best described by the similitude of "two scorpions in a bottle," a metaphor coined by J. Robert Oppenheimer. With further developments in nuclear bombs and greater knowledge of their effects came Dulles's theory of massive nuclear retaliation enunciated in 1954 and

McNamara's flexible response. This was followed by other schools of thought hovering round graduated deterrence, second strike capability, and the oceanic system.

In 1959, Albert Wohlstetter denounced the theory of the "balance of terror." His thesis was that a deterrent force existed only if it was capable of inflicting reprisals. He laid down a set of six conditions for a second strike capability and came to conclude that the United States possessed none of them at that time. Dr. Henry Kissinger, in his famous book *Necessity for Choice,* embraced the new gospel of limited wars and introduced the element of "credibility" to "deterrence." "Deterrence," he wrote, "requires a combination of power, the will to use it, and the assessment of these by the potential aggressor."

Let us now make an attempt to study the Qur'anic concept of strategy. The first step to this study is to understand the difference between total strategy, that is, jihad, and military strategy. The term "jihad," so often confused with military strategy, is, in fact, the near-equivalent of total or grand strategy or policy-in-execution. Jihad entails the comprehensive direction and application of "power," while military strategy deals only with the preparation for and application of "force." Jihad is a continuous and never-ending struggle waged on all fronts, including political, economic, social, psychological, domestic, moral, and spiritual, to attain the object of policy. It aims at attaining the overall mission assigned to the Islamic state, and military strategy is one of the means available to it to do so. It is waged at individual as well as collective level, and at internal as well as external front.

Waged in its true spirit, and with the multiple means available to it, the Islamic concept of total strategy has the capacity to produce direct results. Alternatively, however, it creates conditions conducive to the military strategy to attain its object speedily and economically. Military strategy thus draws heavily on the total strategy (jihad) for its successful application. Any weakness or strength in the formulation, direction, or application of the total strategy would affect military strategy in the like manner. In the absence of jihad, the preparation for and application of "force" to its best advantage would be a matter of exception, not rule. Conversely, optimum preparation and application of the military forms an integral part of jihad.

What then is the Qur'anic concept of military strategy? Instructions pertaining to the divine theory on military strategy are found in the revelations pertaining to the battles of Badr, Ohad, Khandaq, Tabuk, and Hodaibiyya. Recalling the situation at Badr, the Holy Qur'an reminded the Prophet,

> Remember, ye implored the assistance of your Lord and he answered you, "I will assist you with thousands angels, ranks on ranks."

Allah made it but a message of hope and an assurance to your hearts: in any case there is no help except from Allah, and Allah is exalted in power.

Again in the battle of Hunain, the Muslims were initially defeated and faced a situation nearly similar to Ohad, although they recovered soon and won a great victory in the end. Talking of that occasion, the Holy Qur'an says,

> Assuredly, Allah did help you in many battle-fields and on the Day of Hunain: behold! Your great numbers elated you, but they availed you naught: the land, for all that it is wide, did constrain you, and ye turned back in retreat. But Allah did pour his calm on the Apostle and on the believers and sent down forces which ye saw not: He punished the unbelievers.

In the situations referred to above, we see that whenever Almighty Allah wishes to frustrate and destroy the designs of his enemies, he does so by strengthening the hearts of the believers and by sending down calm and tranquility upon them as from himself. We, therefore, infer that, to prevent our adversaries from imposing their will and decision upon us in war, it is essential for us to maintain a state of calm, assurance, hope, and tranquility among our ranks. But what should we do to impose our will and decision upon the enemy? To find answers to this question, let us make another probe into the Book.

Talking of Badr, the Holy Qur'an addresses the Prophet:

> Remember, thy Lord inspired the angels with the message, "I am with you: give firmness to the Believers: I will instill terror into the hearts of the Unbelievers."

Again, in the Battle of Ohad, the Book identified the causes of Muslim defeat and provided them divine guidance about their future course of action. Should the Muslims observe the divine code of conduct prescribed for them, the Book held out a promise, saying,

> Soon shall we cast terror into the hearts of the Unbelievers.

We see that when God wishes to impose his will upon his enemies, he chooses to do so by casting terror into their hearts. But what strategy does he prescribe for the believers to enforce their decision upon their foes?

> Let not the Unbelievers think that they can get the better of the Godly: they will never frustrate them. Against them make ready your strength to the utmost of your power, including steeds of war, to strike terror into the hearts of the enemies of Allah and your enemies, and others besides, whom ye may not know, but whom Allah doth know.

The Qur'anic military strategy thus enjoins us to prepare ourselves for war to the utmost in order to strike terror into the heart of the enemies, known or hidden, while guarding ourselves from being terror-stricken by the enemy. In this strategy, guarding ourselves against terror is the "base"; preparation for war to the utmost is the "cause"; while the striking terror into the hearts of the enemies is the "effect." The whole philosophy revolves round the human heart, his soul, spirit, and faith. In war, our main objective is the opponent's heart or soul, our main weapon of offense against this objective is the strength of our own souls, and to launch such an attack, we have to keep terror away from our own hearts.

The Qur'anic strategy comes into play from the preparation stage, and aims at imposing a direct decision upon the enemy. Other things remaining the same, our preparation for war is the true index of our performance during war. We must aim at creating a wholesome respect for our cause and our will and determination to attain it, in the minds of the enemies, well before facing them on the field of battle. So spirited, zealous, complete, and thorough should be our preparation for war that we should enter upon the "war of muscles" having already won the "war of wills." Only a strategy that aims at striking terror into the hearts of the enemies from the preparation stage can produce direct results and turn Liddell Hart's dream into a reality.

During peacetime, our "will" must find its expression through "preparation." The war of preparation being waged by us during peace is vastly more important than the active war. Strategy has comparatively greater stakes in a drill square, during a training exercise, at a model discussion, and in an operational conference than in the theater or zone of operations. Anything we do or fail to do during peacetime is creating a certain impact—favorable or otherwise—upon our potential adversaries. Seemingly trivial and innocent acts of commission and omission can also accumulate together to assume great importance. We must be constantly conscious of the fact that our strategy is working in full swing during peacetime, and by our actions, we are either contributing toward the attainment of its aim or are undermining it, as the case may be.

Preparation must be "to the utmost," both in quality and in quantity. It must be a continuous and never-ending process. Preparation should be at the plane of total strategy, that is, jihad, and not of the military instrument alone. Military preparedness will yield the desired results only if it forms a part of the total preparedness. Quantitative preparation may have physical limitations but qualitative preparation is limited only by our will and energy to acquire it. The lesser the physical resources, the greater must be the stress and reliance on the spiritual dimensions of war. The operational effectiveness of a fighting force depends upon its total strength: physical as well as spiritual. An army might be inferior in one field but should be superior to the opponent in the aggregate. The side that is inferior in the physical strength can draw on its spiritual strength to acquire a higher degree of aggregate strength. Physical strength must, however, be prepared for and applied "to the utmost." Physical preparedness is complimentary to spiritual preparedness and vice versa; none can compensate or intercede for the other.

Terror struck into the hearts of the enemies is not only a means, it is the end in itself. Once a condition of terror into the opponent's heart is obtained, hardly anything is left to be achieved. It is the point where the means and the ends meet and merge. Terror is not a means of imposing decision upon the enemy; it is the decision we wish to impose upon him.

Psychological and physical dislocation is, at best, a means, though by no means conclusive, for striking terror into the hearts of the enemy. Its effects are related to the physical and spiritual stamina of the opponent but are seldom of a permanent and lasting nature. An army that practices the Qur'anic philosophy of war in its totality is immune to psychological pressures. When Liddell Hart talks of imposing a direct decision upon the enemy through psychological dislocation alone, he is taking too much for granted.

Terror cannot be struck into the hearts of an army by merely cutting its lines of communication or depriving it of its routes of withdrawal. It is basically related to the strength or weakness of the human soul. It can be instilled only if the opponent's faith is destroyed. Psychological dislocation is temporary; spiritual dislocation is permanent. Psychological dislocation can be produced by a physical act but this does not hold true of spiritual dislocation.

To instill terror into the hearts of the enemy, it is essential, in the ultimate analysis, to dislocate his faith. An invincible faith is immune to terror. A weak faith offers inroads to terror. The faith conferred upon us by the Holy Qur'an has the inherent strength to ward off terror and to enable us to strike terror into the enemy. Whatever the form or type of strategy directed against the enemy, it must, in order to be effective, be capable of striking terror into the hearts of the enemy. A strategy that fails to attain this condition suffers from inherent drawbacks and weaknesses and should be reviewed and modified. This rule is fully applicable to nuclear as well as conventional wars. It is equally true of the strategy of nuclear deterrence in fashion today. To be credible and effective, the strategy of deterrence must be capable of striking terror into the hearts of the enemy.

The Conduct of War

To begin this study, let us first recapitulate some of the traditional theories about the conduct of war against the background of which we shall be studying the Qur'anic principles on the subject. In his penetrating work *Strategy: The Indirect Approach*, Liddell Hart made an attempt to extract, from the history of war, a few truths that seemed to him so universal and fundamental as to be termed axioms. According to him, these maxims applied to tactics as well as strategy alike. He came to the general conclusion that all the principles of war could be concentrated into one single principle, that is, concentration of strength against weakness. To apply this principle, he put forward eight rules, six positive and two negative. The positive rules were:

- The maintenance of the aim.
- The adjustment of the means to the end.
- The adoption of the line of least expectation and resistance.
- The undertaking of a line of operations that threatens multiple objectives.
- Ensuring that plans and dispositions are flexible and adaptable to the circumstances.

In the negative rules, he advocated that all the weight should not be thrown in one stroke while the enemy was on guard, and that an attack, once failed, should not be resumed along the same lines or in the same form.

Napoleon emphasized the need for concentration of effort, offensive action, surprise, and protection. Clausewitz evolved two primary rules of war. They were the concentration of effort and action in strength against the main enemy forces, which implied the enforcement of decision in the main theater of operations. In Foch's view, the two decisive rules of warfare were the economy of force and freedom of action. Beaufre agreed with Foch but added that, to apply these rules, it was essential to undertake two progressive steps. The first was to select the decisive point to be attacked; the second, to select the preparatory maneuver that would enable the decisive point to be reached. The champions of the wars of revolution had a different approach to the problem. Lenin and Stalin condensed the theory and practice of war into three main rules. They stressed the unity of the country and the army, the security and protection of the rear areas, and the necessity of psychological action preceding military action. Mao Tse-tung advocated six rules. He recommended concentric withdrawal in face of the enemy advance and advance of his own forces if the enemy withdrew. According to him, strategically, a ratio of one to five was sufficient, but tactically, five to one was essential. He also advocated that there should be close cohesion between the army and the civil population.

In the contemporary thinking on the conduct of war, a high degree of reliance is placed on the principles of war, though the military thinkers do not unanimously agree on one set of principles. The list of the principles put forward from time to time exceeds two dozen but those generally studied in military institutions include:
- Maintenance of the aim.
- Offensive action.
- Concentration.
- Cooperation and coordination.
- Economy of effort.
- Security.
- Morale.
- Administration.
- Unity of command.

The Qur'anic maxims on the conduct of war encompass:
* The art of decision making.
* The supremacy of the aim.
* Selection of objectives.
* Constant striving and struggling.
* Comparative evaluation of situations.
* Domination and aggressiveness.
* Will and determination.
* Patience and perseverance.
* Firmness and steadfastness.
* Sacrifice.
* Unity of thought and action.
* Security and precautions.
* Discipline and obedience.
* Prayers.

Within the overall framework of the Qur'anic concept of the strategy of war, these rules bestow calmness, hope, assurance, and moral ascendancy on the Muslim armies and instill terror into the hearts of the enemy. A brief discussion on each of these rules of war follows in the subsequent paragraphs.

Decision Making
The Book reveals that all decisions pertaining to war must be taken after cool, deliberate, thorough, and detailed deliberation and consultations. Second, the prerogative of the final decision rests with the commander. Third, once taken, the decision must be upheld with single-minded attention and devotion. When everything "human" has gone into the process of decision making, trust must be reposed in God and all fears, doubts, and reservations thrown overboard.

The Supremacy of the Aim
Once the decision is taken, the aim must be kept supreme and uppermost through all the stages of the conduct of war and followed through with utmost zeal. During the Days of Ignorance, the spoils of war and ransom for the prisoners captured during the fighting used to offer great temptation to the belligerents. By a divine injunction, the Holy Qur'an subordinated these temptations to the primary and overriding aim of destroying the enemy. Considerations like the spoils of war and ransom or generosity

Osama bin Laden is shown speaking to reporters in southern Afghanistan in 1998, the same year he threatened a holy war against the West. Writing on behalf of the World Islamic Front, bin Laden issued a fatwa to all Muslims: "The ruling to kill the Americans and their allies—civilians and military— is an individual duty for every Muslim." *(AP/Rahimullah Yousafzai)*

Three years before the attacks on the World Trade Center and the Pentagon, the World Islamic Front called on every Muslim "to comply with God's order to kill the Americans and plunder their money wherever and whenever they find it. We also call on Muslim *ulema*, leaders, youths, and soldiers to launch the raid on Satan's U.S. troops and the devil's supporters allying with them, and to displace those who are behind them so that they may learn a lesson." The terrorist raids of 9/11 claimed the lives of 2,993 (including 19 terrorists) and injured more than 6,290. *(U.S. Navy/Chief Photographer's Mate Eric J. Tilford)*

In the shadow of a portrait of Hasan Al-Banna, Abdullah Farajallah and
Salem al-Falahat of the Muslim Brotherhood join Adnan al-Dulaimi,
then leader of the Iraqi Accordance Front, to celebrate the 100th
anniversary of Al-Banna's birth in Amman, Jordan, on 16 November
2006. Al-Banna founded the Muslim Brotherhood in 1928, at the time
the first mass-based, overtly political movement to oppose the rising
tide of Western ideas in the Middle East. *(AP/Nader Daoud)*

A mentor of Osama bin Laden, Sheikh Abdullah Yusuf 'Azzam was the central figure in the global development of the militant Islamist movement. In his essay, "Join the Caravan," Azzam implores Muslims to rally in defense of Muslim victims of aggression and to restore Muslim lands from foreign domination. Sometimes called "The Godfather of Jihad," he was known for his slogan: "Jihad and the rifle alone: No negotiations, no conferences, and no dialogues." Azzam was assassinated in Peshawar, Pakistan, in November 1989. *(Photo by Al Rai Aam/Feature Story News/Getty Images)*

Masked gunmen, calling themselves the al-Haq Army, surround the
main mosque in Ramadi, Iraq, in June 2005. The armed men blockaded
the mosque to stop city officials and tribal elders who planned a
conference to select representatives to meet with coalition forces.
(AP/Bilal Hussein)

Rocket-propelled grenades, car bombs, and improvised explosive devices (IEDs) are part of the changing tactics used by insurgents in their guerilla war against coalition forces fighting in Iraq. Here, suspected insurgents hold weapons in the streets of Ramadi. *(AP/Bilal Hussein)*

وبغيها على شرائعه وعدائها لعباده المؤمنين.
انهم قد اختاروا سبيل فرعون وقومه وعاد وثمود
As-Sahab

abc

رسالة إلى شعوب الغرب على لسان المجاهد عزام الأمريكي

On the fourth anniversary of the 9/11 attacks, a masked man threatened
terrorist strikes against Los Angeles and Australia on a tape delivered to
ABC News in Pakistan. ABC News reported that the man, purported to be
an American from California, is believed to be an al Qaida member wanted
by the FBI. *(AP via ABC)*

Until his capture in Pakistan in 2006, Syrian Mustafa Setmariam Nasar, also known as Abu Musab al-Suri, was al Qaida's foremost strategic thinker. Al-Suri opened training camps for incoming jihadists in Afghanistan and is believed to have been one of the chief planners behind the 2004 Madrid train bombings and the July 2005 London bombings. His book, *The Call to Global Islamic Resistance*, has been called the *Mein Kampf* of the jihad movement. *(©Handout/epa/Corbis)*

for the prisoners were relegated to a secondary position. They were to be attended to only after the war lays down its burdens, or, alternately, after the Muslims had "thoroughly subdued the land."

Selection of Objectives

On the occasion of the Battle of Badr, the Holy Qur'an issued instructions to the Muslims about the selection of their objectives. "Smite ye above their necks," it said, "and smite all their fingertips off them." The most sensitive parts of the human body lie above the neck. An effective strike against these parts can finish off the opponent totally. At Badr, however, most of the Koraish warriors were wearing armor. The Holy Qur'an counseled the Muslims to smite the finger-tips off such opponents. In battle, therefore, we should first identify and strike at the most sensitive and vulnerable points of our adversary and aim at finishing him off completely. When that is not possible, our effort should be to choose those targets that, when struck, will deprive him of his ability to use his weapons or combat strength against us. We should always avoid hitting the enemy's strength directly with our weakness.

Constant Striving and Struggling

The decision having been taken and the objectives selected, the Book called upon the Muslims to strive and struggle, toward the attainment of the aim, constantly and actively. Striving and struggling implies the spending of one's self in the way of God, either through life or property or both. It demands the pursuit of the aim using multiple and alternative plans, methods, and techniques. Ceaseless but determined, spirited, and thorough efforts launched in the pursuit of the aim are bound to be crowned with success, soon or late. The real test of this virtue, however, comes under conditions of adversity, not prosperity. The struggle must be kept on with full zeal and confidence, whatever the odds.

Comparative Evaluation of Situations

War is an interplay between two or more opposing forces. While assessing or evaluating a military situation, the Holy Qur'an exhorted the Muslims not to remain unmindful of the enemy situation. The ability to locate and exploit the enemy's weaknesses even under adverse circumstances is a supreme act of generalship. The great Muslim general Khalid bin Walid was an expert in this art, and it accounted for many of his brilliant victories.

Successful is the commander who can accurately assess the strength and weakness of his own as well as those of his adversary at all stages of the conduct of war.

Domination and Aggressiveness
The Holy Qur'an wishes to see the Muslim armies always in the uppermost, dominating, and commanding position over those of their adversaries. The Book directed them:

> Then fight and slay the pagans wherever ye find them, and seize them, beleaguer them and lie in wait for them in every stratagem of war.

The Book wants the Muslims to retain the initiative to themselves through bold, aggressive but calculated, and deliberate planning and conduct of war.

Will and Determination
The Qur'anic message on this vitally important issue is that men of faith fighting for a righteous cause with total devotion and submission and willing to make total sacrifice have no cause to fall into despair or weaken in will and determination.

Patience and Perseverance
Scholarly opinion maintains that the book enjoins us not to become rash. It instructs us toward constancy, firmness of purpose and steadfastness. It entails a systematic, as opposed to spasmodic or chance action. It demands a cheerful attitude of resignation and understanding in sorrow, suffering, crisis, or defeat. Patience is an aspect of courage that, in turn, is supported and nourished by professional competence of the highest order. In war, human and equipment casualties will occur, plans will be upset and will need modifications, the frictions of war will upset movement plans, positions will be overrun by the enemy, and attacks will be halted, even repulsed. It will take patience born of professional competence and moral courage to face these situations, and perseverance to attain the goal, tribulations notwithstanding.

Firmness and Steadfastness
Firmness and steadfastness go hand in hand with patience and perseverance. "O ye who believe! Fight the Unbelievers who gird you about,

and let them find firmness in you," was the divine guidance revealed to the Muslims on the eve of the battle of Tabuk. Similar instructions appear in the Book on numerous other occasions. Giving Muslims the divine concept of firmness and steadfastness, the Book says, "Truly Allah loves those who fight in his cause in battle array, as if they were a solid cemented structure." During the conduct of fighting, the Holy Qur'an bade the Muslims never to turn their backs to the enemy, except on two occasions. "O ye who believe!" it directed, "when ye meet the Unbelievers in hostile array, never turn your backs to them. If any do turn his back to them on such a day—unless it be in a stratagem of war, or to retreat to a troop (of his own—he draws on himself the wrath of Allah, and his abode is Hell—an evil refuge [indeed])." The high exceptions recognized were withdrawal as a stratagem of war and the retreat of a detachment of troops to the main body. Allama Abdullah Yousaf Ali interprets stratagem of war as "recuk, pour mieuz Sauter," that is, to go back in order to jump forward or to deceive the enemy by a feint.

Sacrifice

In the Qur'anic perspective, supreme achievement lies in supreme sacrifice. Sacrifice denotes a bond between man and God; in it man sacrifices the ephemeral things of this world to obtain, in return, eternal salvation, the fulfillment of his highest spiritual hopes, which the Holy Qur'an describes as "achievement supreme." Sacrifice may take the form of bearing suffering, hardships, want, hunger, thirst, fatigue, injury, and death. It must be motivated by a selfless spirit of serving the cause. The reward of sacrifice is a life of honor in this world and salvation in the hereafter.

Unity of Thought and Action

During the conduct of fighting, the Holy Qur'an called upon the believers to display the highest standards of mutual love, affection, respect, and concern. It enjoined them to hold together the Rope of God, collectively and firmly, and forge unity and cohesion in their ranks. The Holy Qur'an also warned them to guard against disunity among their ranks. Muslim military history has shown that disunity among the Muslim ranks was one of the biggest factors responsible for our worst defeats. A glaring example is the battle of Tours, fought and lost by the Muslims due to internal strife, in France in AD 732. Except for internal dissension, they stood all chances of winning the battle and changing the entire course of European history in consequence.

Security and Precautions
The Book warns:

> The Unbelievers wish, if ye were negligent of your arms and your baggage, to assault you in a single rush. But there is no blame on you if ye put away your arms because of the inconvenience of rain or because ye are ill; but take every precaution for yourselves.

Discipline and Obedience
Discipline and obedience forms the very heart of Islam, the religion of submission to the will of God. The necessity of willing and instant obedience has been emphasized by the Holy Qur'an on numerous occasions. The discipline and obedience with which Muslims followed their great leader has since become proverbial. While there are innumerable examples of submission and obedience, we must constantly remind ourselves of the fact that it was indiscipline and insubordination of orders that was responsible for the Muslim debacle at Ohad.

Prayers
During the conduct of fighting, the Book calls upon Muslims to resort to prayers more often than in times of peace. The Qur'anic philosophy on the subject is that prayers strengthen faith and protect against psychological pressures.

CHAPTER 7
Join the Caravan

SHEIKH ABDULLAH YUSUF 'AZZAM

Before Osama bin Laden, who was massively influenced by him, Abdullah 'Azzam was the central figure in the global development of the militant Islamist movement. He built the ideological and paramilitary infrastructure for the globalization of Islamic radicalism, which until his arrival on the scene had focused on separate national struggles. 'Azzam's practical approach to the recruitment and training of Muslim militants from around the world blossomed during the Afghan war against the Soviets and provided the cadres and infrastucture from which al Qaida was created and supported.

'Azzam's radical ideology, combined with his skill at organizing paramilitary training for more than twenty thousand Muslim recruits from about twenty countries around the world, created an international cadre of highly motivated and experienced militants intent on perpetuating his vision of global Islamic revolution. In Join the Caravan, *he implores Muslims to rally in defense of Muslim victims of aggression, to restore Muslim lands from foreign domination, and to uphold the Muslim faith. His trademark slogan was "Jihad and the rifle alone: no negotiations, no conferences, and no dialogues."*

Reasons for Jihad

Anybody who looks into the state of Muslims today will find that their greatest misfortune is their abandonment of jihad due to their love of this world and hatred of death. Because of that, the tyrants have gained dominance over Muslims in every aspect and in every land. The reason for this is that the disbelievers only stand in awe of fighting. We then are calling upon the Muslims and urging them to proceed to fight, for many reasons, at the head of which are the following:

1. In order that the disbelievers do not dominate.
2. Due to the scarcity of men.
3. Fear of the hellfire.
4. Fulfilling the duty of jihad, and responding to the call of the Lord.
5. Following in the footsteps of the predecessors.
6. Establishing a solid foundation as a base for Islam.
7. Protecting those who are oppressed in the land.
8. Hoping for martyrdom and a high station in paradise.

In Order That the Disbelievers Do Not Dominate
In the noble verse of the Qur'an, we find: "And fight them until *fitnah* [polytheism] is no more, and the Religion is entirely for Allah. But if they desist, Allah sees what they do." So, if the fighting stops, the disbelievers will dominate, and *fitnah*, which is *shirk* (polytheism), will spread.

Due to the Scarcity of Men
The crisis of the Muslim world is the lack of men who are competent in bearing responsibility and meriting trust, as has been reported in Saheeh al-Bukhari: "People are like a hundred camels out of which you can hardly find one suitable to ride." This means that the ultimate in moderation regarding things of this world and in longing for the hereafter is as scarce as a mount. The men who know are few; those who act are even fewer. Those who perform jihad are rarer still, and those who remain steadfast on this path are hardly sufficient to be mentioned. Many a time have I looked in on a gathering for Qur'anic recitation, comprising Arab youths who came to the Land of Honor and Glory—by which I mean the land of Afghanistan. I am saying that I have looked at the countenances of the youths, seeking one among them proficient in the rules of Qur'anic reci-

tation so that I could put him in charge of the group, but I did not find a single such person.

We are saying that our learned brethren and mature propagators have not come to us. On the contrary, some of them even advise those who come forward to sit complacently in their own countries, even if they could not say a word against the injustice of the oppressors and the tyranny of the occupiers. And some of them give verdicts without knowledge, saying, "The Afghans are in need of money and not in need of men." As for me, through the course of my day-to-day life for this jihad, I have found that the Afghans are in severe need of money. But their need for men is more severe, and the need of propagators is even greater.

If you have any doubt about what I am saying, then come with us. We will pass through Afghanistan so that you can see for yourself an entire regiment in which not a single person among them is proficient in the recitation of the Qur'an. Then move on with me to another regiment so that you can be convinced that there is nobody in it who knows how to perform the funeral prayer, on account of which they are forced to carry their martyrs long distances in order to find somebody to pray over his body. As for the juristic details of the jihad, such as the distribution of booty and treatment of prisoners of war, these matters have arisen in many regiments. Due to ignorance about them, however, they were forced to pass them on to an area in which there was a scholar or scholars who could give the decisions according to the Islamic law. You will become aware of the Arab youths' modest education (possibly not even surpassing secondary school), of the severe need for propagators, imams, reciters of the Qur'an, and religious scholars.

Fear of the Hellfire
Allah, the mighty, the majestic, says: "Unless you march forth, he will punish you with a severe punishment, and will replace you with another people." It has been said that what is meant by this verse is that going on jihad is compulsory in times of need.

Al-Bukhari tells about the unfaithful Muslims who went over to the enemy before the Battle of Badr and were killed, and according to Al-Bukhari's narration, they deserve hell. What then do you think about the millions of Muslims who are being humiliated with dreadful persecution and are living the lives of cattle? They cannot repel attacks on their honor, lives, and properties. Nay, such a man cannot even have his own way in growing his beard because it is an obvious sign of Islam. Nor, in fact, is he free to have his wife wear the long garments required by Islam because it is a crime for which he may be seized anywhere and at any time. Nor can he teach the Qur'an to three Muslim youths in the mosque because it is an illegal gathering according to the law of the ignorant. Nay, in some of the countries that are called Islamic, he cannot even have his wife cover her hair, nor can he prevent the intelligence officers from taking his daughter by the hand in the depths of night, under the cover of pitch darkness, to wherever they wish. Are these millions not living lives of despicable subjugation, and do the angels not take their souls while they are wronging themselves? Weakness is not an excuse before the Lord. In fact, it is a crime that deserves hell. But Allah has excused those of advanced years, the small children, and the women who neither find any scheme for liberation nor know the path to the Land of Honor, nor are able to emigrate to the land of Islam or to arrive at the base for jihad.

Jihad has a deep-rooted role that cannot be separated from the constitution of this religion. A religion that does not have jihad cannot become established in any land, nor can it strengthen its frame. Jihad is one of the innermost constituents of this religion and is not a contingent phenomenon peculiar to the period in which the Qur'an was revealed. It is in fact a necessity accompanying the caravan that this religion guides.

Responding to the Call of the Lord
Allah, Most High, says, "March forth, whether light or heavy, and fight with your wealth and your lives in the path of Allah; that is better for you, if only you knew." The correct interpretation of this is that people have been ordered as a whole to go forth, whether the activity required of that person is light or heavy. A sensible person does not doubt that the conditions in which we are living, in Afghanistan and Palestine—nay, in the major part of the Muslim world—fall under the jurisdiction of this verse.

There is agreement among scholars that when the enemy enters an Islamic land or a land that was once part of the Islamic lands, it is obligatory on the inhabitants of that place to go forth to face the enemy. But if they sit back, or are incapable, lazy, or insufficient in number, the individual obligation spreads to those around them. Then if they also fall short or sit back, it goes to those around them, and so on and so on, until the individually obligatory nature of jihad encompasses the whole world. At that time, nobody can abandon it to the extent that the son may go out without the permission of his father, the debtor without the permission of the one he owes, the woman without the permission of her husband, and the slave without the permission of his master. The individually obligatory nature of jihad remains in effect until the lands are purified from the pollution of the disbelievers. However, a woman going out on a journey must have a *mahram* [male relative she is forbidden to marry].

Following the Predecessors
Jihad was a way of life for the predecessors, and the Prophet was a model for the mujahideen and for inexperienced people. When there was fierce fighting, they used to stand resolutely by the Prophet lest he be closest to the enemy. The total number of military excursions that he accompanied was twenty-seven, and he himself fought in nine of these. This means that the Prophet used to go out on military expeditions or send out an army at least every two months. The companions continued upon the path of the Prophet and brought up a generation with an education of jihad. They had been bathed in jihad and cleansed of engrossment in worldly matters, just as a wound is bathed in water.

There are the handful of military officers, some of whom may think that it is possible for them to carry out a collective Muslim effort—this is a kind of fantasy or delusion, reminiscent of the past. It will be no more than a repetition of the tragedy of Abdul Nasser with the Islamic movement once again. The popular jihad movement, with its long path of effort, great sacrifice, and serious losses, purifies souls so that they tower above the lower material world. Important matters rise above petty disputes about money, short-term desires, and inferior provisions. Malice disappears and souls are sharpened; and the caravan moves on from the foot of the mountain up to the lofty summit, far away from the stench of clay and the struggles of low ground. Along the path of jihad, the leadership is categorized, abilities become manifest from the offerings and sacrifices, and men come forth with bravery and service.

When important matters are the only concern, souls are uplifted above minor issues, and important things occupy people's hearts and hopes. When you embark on an honorable venture, be not content with aiming below the stars. For death in a paltry matter is like the death in a significant matter. The cowards will see cowardice as reason, and that is the treachery of the depraved disposition.

The nature of societies is precisely that of water. In stagnant water, water moss and decayed matter float on the surface, whereas flowing water will not carry scum on its surface. Similarly, the leadership of a stagnant society cannot fulfill its responsibility because leadership emerges only through movement, sacrifice, service, and offering. The *ummah* that performs jihad pays a high price, and so it harvests ripe fruits. It is not easy to lose something that was won through sweat and blood, but whoever seized a land without war, it is easy for him to surrender that land.

The *ummah* of jihad, which is led by extraordinary people who emerged through the long jihad movement, will not easily lose command, nor serve as easy prey for collapse. It is also not easy for its enemies to make it harbor suspicions about its heroes' excursions. The jihad movement familiarizes the *ummah* with all its individuals, informing it that they have contributed to the price paid and have participated in the sacrifice for the establishment of the Islamic state. Thus they will be trustworthy custodians of this new-born state, which will relieve the entire *ummah* from the agony of its labor pains. Without a doubt, the Islamic state will be born, but birth cannot be accomplished without labor, and with labor there must be pain.

Protecting the Oppressed in the Land
Among the incentives for the Islamic jihad is the protection of those who are weak and oppressed in the land, and lifting injustice off them. How can there be relaxation, and how can the Muslims be calm, when Muslim women are with the oppressing enemy?

The Islamic jurists are in consensus that jihad becomes an individual obligation both physically and by material support, when a Muslim woman is taken captive. I wish that, even if they will not protect the religion, at least, they would fight defending the woman's honor. Even if they are not interested in jihad's reward, they could, at least, come and fight to win booty.

Once I was with Hikmatyar, in Logar [a province of Afghanistan], when he struck a serious blow to the Communist headquarters of the province. The children of the province shouted, and the tongues of the women were full of prayers for Hikmatyar. Are Muslim women being taken captive in every land? Shall the lives of Muslims then be comfortable? Do Allah and Islam not have the right that every youth and aged one should fight for it?

Hoping for Martyrdom and a High Station in Paradise
It has been reported in the authentic Hadith: "The martyr has seven special favors from Allah":
- He is forgiven his sins with the first spurt of his blood.
- He sees his place in paradise before his soul leaves his body.
- He is clothed with the garment of faith.
- He is wed with seventy-two wives from the beautiful maidens of paradise.
- He is saved from the punishment of the grave.
- He is protected from the great terror of the Day of Judgment.
- On his head is placed a crown of dignity, a jewel of which is better than the world and all it contains.
- He is granted intercession for seventy people of his household.

Al-Bukhari has reported that the Prophet said, "In Paradise there are one hundred levels that Allah has prepared for the mujahideen; the difference between every pair of these is like the difference between heaven and earth." Indeed, jihad is a shield for the *ummah*'s honor, and a means for lifting disgrace off them.

O'Islam!

The enormous sacrifices apportioned to the Afghan Muslim people are no secret to you. To date, nine years and some have passed since the start of the illustrious revolution against the Communist invasion. During this time, Muslims in Afghanistan have endured as much as mortals can endure in the course of protecting their religion, honor, and children. Not a single house remains in Afghanistan that has not been transformed into a funeral home or an orphanage.

These people have an excuse before Allah, and have called to Allah to bear witness, on the basis of their skulls, cripples, souls, and blood, that there has not remained a single arrow in the bow, and the arrows of the quiver have almost broken through. Through the course of this long period of time, the Afghans had expectations of their Muslim brethren in case their numbers became decreased, and also so that the Muslim brotherhood could be aroused in their midst. Yet until now, the Muslims have not heeded their call. In the ears of the Muslims is a silence, rather than the cries of anguish, the screams of virgins, the wails of orphans, and the sighs of old men. Many well-off people have deemed it sufficient to send some of the scraps from their tables and crumbs from their food.

But the situation is more serious, and gravely momentous, and the Muslims in Afghanistan are in severe distress and definite, menacing peril. This blessed jihad was established by a handful of youths who were nurtured in Islam, and by a group of scholars who devoted themselves to Allah. However, most of this first generation has fallen in martyrdom, and the second generation has advanced. This second generation has not been fortunate enough to receive the same share of upbringing and guidance, and has not come across an outstretched hand showing an interest in teaching and training them. Such people are in dire need of somebody who can live among them to direct them toward Allah and teach them religious regulations.

According to our modest experience and knowledge, we believe that jihad in the present situation in Afghanistan is individually obligatory, with one's self and wealth as has been confirmed by the jurists of the four schools of Islamic jurisprudence, without any exception. Jihad is obligatory on every individual according to his capability and wealth, little or plenty, whether walking or riding. When the enemy proceeded toward the Muslims in the Battle of the Trench, Allah did not excuse anybody. The texts of the four juristic schools are explicit and definite in this respect and leave no room for interpretation, ambiguity, or uncertainty.

Perhaps some people find justification for themselves for avoiding jihad by the fact that many of the Afghans are not at an acceptable level of Islamic upbringing, and they therefore make excuses for themselves, on the basis of some irregularities, to sit back. But the refutation of this is that the jurists have documented that it is obligatory to perform jihad even with an extremely sinful army. This is one of the principles of Ahlus-Sunnah wal-Jamah, to "perform jihad with every pious and sinful man," for Allah will support this religion through a sinful man, and by means of disgraceful people who have no morals. Some others excuse themselves by claiming that their presence in their country is necessary for the purpose of education and upbringing. For such people, we present the words of Az-Zuhri: "Al-Musayyib went out to battle at the point where he had lost the use of one of his eyes. He was told, 'You are an invalid,' but he said, 'Allah has summoned forth the light and the heavy. So if I cannot fight, I will swell the ranks and guard belongings.'" Matters have reached a critical point, the noose is tightening, the situation is grave for the Muslims, so when will we go forth? And for how long will we sit back doing nothing? What would our scholars say about the thousands of women who are being raped in their homes? How would they respond to the women who cast themselves in the Kunar River in Laghman, fleeing from rape at the hands of the Red Army, in order to guard their chastity? Do you not fear that your turn may come, and that the matter will concern your own honor? The Russians have taken 5,200 Afghan Muslim children to rear them on the Communist ideology, and to sow heresy deep within them. The Americans have confirmed the opening of six hundred schools, and they are maintaining, educating, and raising 150,000 Afghan children inside and outside the country. Where then are the propagators of Islam? Where are the Muslim educators and what have they prepared for saving this Muslim generation and for safeguarding this great and blessed people? The jurists have documented that the lands of the Muslims are like a single land, so that whichever region of the Muslims' territory is exposed to danger, it is necessary that the whole body of the Islamic *ummah* rally together to protect this organ that is exposed to the onslaught of the microbe. What is the matter with the scholars, that they do not arouse the youths for jihad, especially since arousal is compulsory? What is the matter with the propagators that they do not dedicate a year of their lives to live among the mujahideen, giving guidance and direction? What is the matter with the students that they do not take a year off from their studies in order to attain the distinction of jihad and contribute with their own selves to the establishment of Allah's religion on earth? What is the matter with the imams, that they do not sincerely advise those who seek counsel from them regarding going out with blood and soul in the path of Allah? For how long will the believing youths be held back and restrained from jihad? These youths, whose hearts are burning with a fire, spurting forth enthusiasm, and blazing with zeal that their pure blood may irrigate the earth of the Muslims. The one who forbids a young man from jihad is no different from the one who forbids him from prayer and fasting. What is the matter with the mothers, that one of them does not send forward one of her sons in the path of Allah, that he might be a pride for her in this world and a treasure for her in the hereafter through his intercession? And what is the matter with the fathers that they do not urge one of their sons, so that he can grow up in the rearing-ground of heroes, the lands of men and the grounds of battle? He should consider that Allah created him infertile, and part of giving thanks for the blessing of children is to submit the charity from his children as thanks to his Lord. Did he create himself or provide himself with wealth? Why then, the stinginess toward the Lord? So the bloody tale of Bukhara, the narrative of mutilated Palestine, blazing Aden, enslaved peoples, the sorry stories of Spain, the terrible accounts of Eritrea, sore Bulgaria, the tragedy of Sudan, the devastated remnants of Lebanon, Somalia, Caucasia, and its deep wounds, Uganda, Zanzibar, Indonesia, Nigeria . . . all these slaughters and tragedies are the best lesson for us. Will we take admonishment from the past before we lose the present? Or will history repeat itself over us while we swallow degradation, fall into oblivion as those before us did, and lose just as they lost? We hope that Allah defeats the Russians in Afghanistan, and that the Muslims do not turn back on their heels in failure.

Conclusion

1. When the enemy enters the land of the Muslims, jihad becomes individually obligatory (Fard Ain), according to all the jurists.
2. When jihad becomes obligatory for all, there is no difference between it and fasting, according to the three imams.
3. When jihad becomes obligatory on all, no permission of parents is required, just as parents' permission is not required to fast at Ramadan.
4. There is no difference between one who abandons jihad without excuse when it is obligatory and one who eats without excuse during the day in Ramadan.
5. Donating money does not exempt a person from bodily jihad, no matter how great the amount of money given. Nor is the obligation of jihad, which is hanging over the person's neck, lifted from him; just as it is not correct to give money to the poor for missed fasts or prayers without making them up.
6. Jihad is the obligation of a lifetime, just like fasting. As it is not permissible to fast one year in Ramadan and eat in the following Ramadan, or to pray one day and abandon prayer another day, similarly one cannot perform jihad one year and abandon it for some years if he is capable of continuing.
7. Jihad is currently obligatory for every individual—in person and by wealth, in every place that the disbelievers have occupied. It remains obligatory continuously until every piece of land that was once Islamic is regained.

8. The word "jihad," when mentioned on its own, only means combat with weapons, as was mentioned by Ibn Rushd, and upon this the four imams have agreed.
9. The implication of being in the path of Allah is jihad.
10. The saying, "We have returned from the lesser jihad (battle) to the greater jihad," which people quote on the basis that it is a hadith, is in fact a false, fabricated hadith that has no basis. It is only a saying of Ibrahim bin Abi Ablah, one of the successors, and it contradicts textual evidence and reality.
11. Jihad is the highest peak of Islam and proceeds in stages—preparation, organization, then combat.
12. Jihad today is individually obligatory, by self and wealth, on every Muslim, and the Muslim *ummah* remains sinful until the last piece of Islamic land is freed from the hands of the disbelievers. Furthermore, none are absolved from the sin other than the mujahideen.
13. Allah has not excused anybody to abandon jihad other than the ill, the cripple, and the blind, as well as children who have not yet reached puberty, women who have no way of emigrating and performing jihad, and those advanced in years. In fact, it is better for even the sick person whose illness is not serious, as well as the cripple and the blind person, if they are able to make their way to the training camps in order to join the mujahideen, teach them Qur'an, talk to them, and encourage them to be brave. Anybody else has no excuse before Allah, whether he is a professional, a specialist, an employer, or a great businessman. None of these is excused from performing jihad personally or permitted to merely contribute materially.
14. Jihad is a collective act of worship, and every group must have a leader. Obedience to the leader is a necessity in jihad, and thus a person must condition himself to invariably obey the leader, as has been reported in the Hadith: "You must hear and obey, whether it is easy or difficult for you, in things which are pleasant for you as well as those which are inconvenient and difficult for you."

Notes for Those Coming for Jihad

1. The jihad of ordinary people is different from the jihad of Islamic propagators. The propagators are always few, and as a rule they are the prime of the *ummah*. They alone cannot continue a prolonged jihad,

nor are they capable of confronting nations, and so the *ummah* must participate with them.

2. The Afghan people are like any other people in that there is ignorance and shortcomings among them, so let not anybody think that he will find an entire people without any deficiencies. However, the difference between the Afghan people and others is that the Afghans have refused disgrace in their religion and have purchased their dignity with seas of blood and mountains of corpses and lost limbs. Other nations have submitted to colonization and disbelief from the first day.

3. The Afghan nation is illiterate and has been reared only on the Hanafi school of thought. No other school of jurisprudence has coexisted with the Hanafi school in Afghanistan and thus many of them think that anything that contradicts the Hanafi school is not part of Islam. The absence of other juristic schools in Afghanistan has led to partisanship and prejudice in favor of the Hanafi school in the hearts of the Afghan people. Therefore anybody who wishes to perform jihad with the Afghans should respect the Hanafi school.

4. The Afghans are a faithful people who recognize manhood, chivalry, and pride and do not appreciate trickery or hypocrisy. When they love a person, they will give their life and soul for him, and if they dislike him they will not show it at all. A person should desist from certain actions of the prayer when he first mingles with them, in order to give himself a valuable chance of reaching their hearts so that he will be able to instruct and educate them and thus improve their worldly and religious conditions.

5. You should certainly know that the path of jihad is long and arduous and that it is not easy for most people to remain steadfast on the journey even if they were very eager at the start. Many youth came here zealous, but then their zeal steadily diminished until they began disputing the very ordinance of jihad. Allah has undertaken to support the mujahideen, so whoever goes forth in his path, Allah will guide him, strengthen his determination, fortify his heart, and make his feet firm.

Clarifications about the Issue of Jihad Today

1. We have spoken at length about the status of jihad today in Afghanistan, Palestine, and other usurped Muslim lands of the like.

2. The obligation of jihad today remains an individual obligation on all until the liberation of the last piece of land that was in the hands of Muslims but has been occupied by the disbelievers.
3. Some scholars consider jihad today in Afghanistan and Palestine to be a communal obligation for local Muslims. We agree with them in that jihad in Afghanistan for the Arabs was initially a communal obligation. However, the jihad is in need of men, and the inhabitants of Afghanistan have not met the requirement, which is to expel the disbelievers from Afghanistan. In this case, the communal obligation is overturned and has become individually obligatory, and remains so until enough mujahideen have gathered to expel the Communists.
4. There is no permission needed from anybody in the case of an individual obligation.
5. A person who discourages people from jihad is like the one who discourages people from fasting. Whoever advises an able Muslim not to go for jihad is just like the one who advises him to eat in Ramadan while he is healthy and in residence.
6. It is best to shun the company of those who hold back from jihad and not to enter into arguments with them, for this would lead to idle disputation and hardening of the heart.

Adding to the Texts of Scholars Already Mentioned

Those with valid excuses are absolved of the sin of sitting back from jihad. Those legitimately excused include:

A. Somebody with a wife and children who do not have income from any other source nor have anybody besides him who could support and maintain them. However, if he is able to allocate provision for them for the duration of his absence, then he is sinful if he sits back. Every Muslim should reduce his spending and be frugal with his earnings until he is able to go out for jihad.
B. Somebody who was unable, after much effort, to obtain a visa to come to Pakistan.
C. Somebody whose government denied him a passport or prevented him from leaving from the airport.
D. Somebody who has parents who do not have anybody besides him for their support and maintenance.

The Question of Interrogation by Authorities upon Return of the Mujahid to His Homeland from Jihad

This point is never an excuse because it is a matter of suspicion and uncertainty. Jihad is a certainty and the fear of interrogation by the intelligence services is a matter of doubt. In fact, even if he is certain that the intelligence services will interrogate him, this is not an excuse that absolves him from the sin of sitting back from jihad. The excuse of coercion that is admissible in the sharia and would absolve him of the sin of abandoning an obligation is "direct coercion that threatens loss of life or limb," that is, torture involving death or severance of a limb. Similarly, fear of police authorities in the country whose passport he holds, even if he is sure that when he returns they will detain him and kill him or sever his limb, is not an acceptable excuse before Allah because in this case he is obliged to forsake his country and live in the land of jihad.

The Issue of Arab Women Performing Jihad in Afghanistan

Arab women may not come without a nonmarriageable male guardian. Their duties are confined to education, nursing, and assisting refugees. As for fighting, Arab women may not fight because, until now, Afghan women are not participating in the fighting.

The Issue of Somebody Who Has a Handicap (Such as the Cripple) That Prevents Him from Fighting but Does Not Prevent Him from Working in Other Spheres

The individual obligation is not dismissed from a cripple or from an invalid whose illness is not serious, because they are capable of working in the spheres of health and education, which is a broad field. The mujahideen are now more in need of propagators than they are in need of food, weapons, and medicine. Therefore, if going out to swell the ranks is obligatory, then how about going out to teach the mujahideen the regulations of their religion? This is more obligatory and more strongly compulsory.

A Word to Those with Families

In conclusion: We tell those with families that they may not leave their families and go out for jihad without ensuring provision for them and without ensuring that somebody will take care of them. Thus, whoever wishes to go out now with his family should realize that we are not able to take care of him. He should therefore check with the Islamic centers close to him or with well-wishers until he is able to guarantee provision for his family. The poor people with families must therefore determinedly look for somebody who can financially support their families for the duration of their absence. They should urgently hasten to take care of their financial affairs, then go out for jihad. "The jihad is in need of money, and men are in need of jihad."

CHAPTER 8
Bush under the Microscope

ABU-'UBAYD AL-QURASHI

There is nothing available in open sources as to who al-Qurashi is, except that he has written a series of columns for jihadist Web sites and publications that have garnered a large audience. Many believe he writes under a pen name, and because he has not published anything since 2006 there is speculation that he has been captured or killed. His short article is included here because it is instructive on how the jihadists use reporting by Western media to paint a bleak picture of Western society and its leadership, and how the media is used to lift the terrorists' morale and recruiting efforts.

P olitical psychology is a science concerned with the role that human thinking, feeling, and behavior play in policy. It leads its engaged practitioners to search for social and psychological backgrounds in order to understand the political process and the particulars it subsumes, such as decision making, persuasion, the art of leadership, collective behavior, and cooperation and conflict. Very sadly, our enemies have showed the most interest in this subject, and by means of it they have realized many of their objectives. The Islamic movements, on the other hand, have neglected it in general and in detail, either because of ignorance of its importance or because of Islamic reservations about psychology in principle.

The Importance of Political Psychology

It is not our concern here to criticize the distorted nature of some of these theories. Rather, we are concerned with stating what deserves interest in the mass of information that political psychology itself contains, especially the psychological profiling of political leaders.

The existing literature on the subject takes the form of a quantitative investigation or a qualitative investigation. A quantitative investigation usually seeks to compare a particular political leader with others throughout history. A qualitative investigation seeks to establish a psychological description of the personality of a particular political leader through what has been written about him, what he has written about himself, the testimony of people who have lived close to him, newspaper interviews with him, and so forth. This qualitative investigation in fact makes it possible to assemble an integrated picture of the personality under study and then to understand the nature of the positions to which it commits itself and the decisions that it makes.

The Zionists early realized the importance of this field and made every effort to understand every aspect of it. The result was that they used this branch of learning on the domestic front. Because the Zionist entity consisted and still consists of human assemblages lacking identity, the leaders of the Zionist entity tried to profit as much as possible from political psychology to shape Zionistically desirable political attitudes and positions among the members of incoming groups. On the external front, psychology was effectively used to shape tools of psychological warfare against enemies. In this context, the psychological study of leaders, both hostile and friendly, was a subject of the highest interest among the Zionists.

For example, the Zionists' knowledge of the psychology of American President Johnson, due to the infiltration of his administration by Zionist elements, was one of the basic factors behind the enormous and unlimited support that the Zionists received from America during the 1967 war. Political psychology also was among the factors that drove Egypt into the clutches of humiliation and surrender: A Zionist professor had analyzed the personality of the late President Anwar al-Sadat and discovered its points of imbalance. Al-Sadat, for many reasons, was thoroughly absorbed in an inferiority complex. Realizing that exaggerated praise would be the easiest way to get what they wanted from him, the Zionists inaugurated an intensive media campaign portraying al-Sadat as a man of peace, even

the greatest man of the century, and other such hoaxes! They stepped up
this media campaign until it was impossible for a month to go by in the
late seventies without al-Sadat's picture occupying the middle of the front
pages of the major international newspapers and magazines. As expected,
al-Sadat swallowed the bait and signed the treaty of surrender at Camp
David. He soon gave his life as its price, while the Zionist professor
who analyzed his personality received the highest medals from former
American president Carter's administration. How else, when he was the
one who helped remove Egypt from the arena of conflict in the Middle
East merely by a psychological study!

Since that time, political psychology has been enlisted at every opportunity to damage any foe of America or of the Zionist entity. In is no
wonder in this regard that many studies have been published about the
psychology of Saddam and Arafat, for example, in the context of preparing
the atmosphere for their removal. However, the other Arab rulers, whose
psychologies carry only God knows how many flaws, have not had the
lights focused on them, as long as they remained in the service of their
masters as desired.

Inasmuch as the leaders of America have surpassed others for decades
in using political psychology in peace and in war, the time has come to
take an interest in this subject, so that the enemies of Islam, headed by
the leaders of America, can in turn be put under the microscope. Then
the truth about the great men of the most powerful state on the face of the
earth will become visible to Muslims. It will become clear to everyone
that all the majesty, grandeur, honors, and protocols rendered to them
are merely cosmetics to beautify a group of people who are nothing but
deluded and psychologically ill.

Theoretical Approach

We shall limit ourselves in this article to choosing the American president
George Bush as a unit of analysis, although others are more deserving of
interest because they hold the real keys of government and likewise have
psychological symptoms deserving study: for example, Vice President
Cheney, Secretary of Defense Rumsfeld, and Presidential Advisor for
National Security Affairs Rice. This means that this team is marked with
a particular psychological character reflected in its decisions, rendering it
easy to see the direction in which it is going.

Although the power of the American presidency is limited theoretically by the prerogatives of Congress, and so forth, and this president's penumbra in particular is more limited because of his weak education and political experience, forcing him to defer constantly to his advisors' opinions, a study of his psychology is necessary in order to know the reasons why these powerful lobbies selected this particular person at this particular time.

The theoretical approach employed will rely on defining the personality as "a constant group of attitudes and traits that determine public and private matters in the psychic behavior of persons (thoughts, feelings, actions) and that have an extension in time unrelated to accidental social or biological pressures." The theory followed in the analysis holds that the personality is composed of three reference points: the core of the personality (things that are common to all people), the personal periphery (repeated behaviors, traits of habitual nature, general attitudes of the personality), and personal development (acquired attributes). In our case, we shall consider the second and third points most important.

Analysis of the Data Relating to Bush's Personality

The Distinctive Traits of Bush's Personality
Clowning

One of the most prominent symptoms present in Bush's personality is what can be described as clownish conduct. This kind of behavior has escaped from Bush on dozens of official and other occasions.

- In 1999, a terrible mass murder took place in a church, with eight persons killed. During the official funeral, Bush attended in his capacity as governor of Texas to console the victims' relatives. However, rather than dignity as his prominent trait on that day, out of respect for the feelings of the victims and their families, Bush's first concern was to exchange broad smiles and joke from a distance with some of the reporters in a boyish manner previously unfamiliar to any of them.

- On another occasion, a film producer accompanied Bush on a long election trip by train. The documentary film was more than telling. Bush would sometimes wink at every official. At other times he would behave childishly, shuffling papers and overturning cups. He sometimes danced in imitation of a female dancer. At other times he ate with his mouth open to imitate certain animals. And this was while he was in a heated race to win the presidency of the United States! Just imagine!

As psychology recognizes, childish behavior is one of the symptoms of passive-aggressive personality disorder. The person with this disorder tries to take revenge on things he does not accept in his personality by resorting to this kind of behavior. It means that the person has poor self-esteem. Recurrent psychological crises and alcoholism therefore are some of the traits linked to this personality. As is well known, these are things present in Bush's personality.

Passivity

This characteristic can be considered one of the ingrained traits of Bush's personality. Since childhood he has allowed others to manage his life, especially the important turning points. In fact, Bush senior was the guiding mind of all the details great and small of Bush junior's life. In return, Bush junior did not bother to make any decisions about his future as long as he continued to enjoy the social prestige that his father's name gave him. For example, Bush junior was well received at Andover Academy, the same preparatory school where his father studied and that usually admits only superior students. Although Bush junior was not such a student, his father's name opened doors and hearts to him, as has been noted by his friend from that time, Bill Semple. The same thing happened when Bush senior forced his son to enter Yale to study law. Although Bush junior was as far as could be from the field, he was forced to study there. Accordingly, he was not at all known for excellence or superiority. Indeed, Bush junior proudly boasts about his bad academic past in one of his speeches. In one of his speeches two years ago, when he saw his colleague William Buckley praising him as "one of the superior ones," Bush said, "We have many things in common: William wrote a book while he was studying at college, and I read a book; he founded a political party, and I launched many dances."

The passivity continued until he became president. Because he knows nothing about foreign policy, the main cabinet secretaries and advisors are the real decision makers, while Bush repeats what he is asked to like a parrot.

This passivity may be the most important key to understanding Bush junior's success in winning the presidency. That is because he left everything in his father's hands, to manage as the latter wished and to satisfy through him his clique and friends. Otherwise, as the historian J. H. Hatfield has stated, he would never have had any influence worth mentioning.

We therefore are faced with an example of a pampered child who waits for his father to provide everything he wants from him, from the simplest things to the presidency of the United States of America; and this is what has really happened.

From the foregoing, one can deduce that Bush suffers from the symptoms of dependent personality disorder. These are symptoms accompanied by the following manifestations:

- Inability to make decisions without the exaggerated backing of others.
- Always agreeing with others, despite the certainty that they are wrong.
- Inability to start any valuable action without the help of others. (One should note here that all of Bush junior's successful business dealings would not have taken place without his father's direct or indirect support.)
- Readiness to commit bad acts to win the love of some people.
- A sense of great injury upon encountering criticism.

Sadism

The presence of sadism in Bush's personality may surprise some, but the truth is that many of Bush's actions confirm this turn. For example, the *New York Times* revealed in the mid-sixties how Bush had been a member of Delta Kappa Epsilon fraternity, a fraternity that engages in sadistic ceremonies toward new college pledges, such as beating, torture, humiliation, and so on. The ceremonies are meant to "force" the new pledges to honor the old members. A related matter that deserves mention is that Bush got into legal difficulties at this time for destroying installations on a football field. The only motive for the action was to deprive the users of the field of the chance to engage in their favorite sport. Bush at this time is also known to have harassed women while driving his car as if going to a hunting trip.

Among other manifestations of sadism in Bush are his love of coarse language, his encouragement of torture (Guantanamo, for example), and his delight in expressions of war and violence. He is fond of being photographed without any motive with a gun in his hand. Actually, he is a coward whom his father rescued from military service in Vietnam by keeping him with the Reserves in Texas. Impatient with the Reserves, he soon boarded the first plane to accompany former president Nixon's daughter Tricia on a romantic tour. It really was the crime of deserting military service and was punishable by law, though not against the son of the director of the CIA.

Nevertheless, Bush junior boasts of having signed more death sentences that any other state governor. These are all signs of the undoubted presence of sadism in Bush's personality.

The Functional Characteristics of Bush's Personality

Working under Pressure

As became clear to millions of observers, Bush junior was by no means of the required stature during the attack of September 11. He was so surprised by its occurrence that, questioned about his feelings, he wept before the cameras. He hid from view for a week, during which time the mayor of New York acted as if he were the real president of the United States. Then the episode of "the terrorist cookie," whose story Bush invented and whose incidents he made up, revealed Bush returning to his favorite hobby, alcoholism. This means that Bush has no strength to deal with crises and no capacity for them.

Intellectual Perception

As has already become clear, Bush does not possess extraordinary intellectual powers—quite the opposite. His education is very limited, and his perception of the external word stops at a few generalities. This is a matter that the European rulers, and later their press, have discovered. Contrary to what may appear when Bush memorizes his speeches well, he makes many simple mistakes in language. This was apparent in his interview with the Associated Press in 2001, when he pronounced his notorious sentence: "There is [sic] madmen in the world, and there are terror." The confusion of singular and plural was something even a child would not fall into. Psychologists have explained this factor as a flaw in the personality.

Entertainment

As is well known, Bush junior has led a life full of immorality and debauchery. His favorite pastime was to drink alcohol with his friend Clay Johnson for three successive days a week at the Midland Country Club.

As a result, by the time Bush reached forty, he had become addicted to alcohol, unable to get away from the bottle at home or on trips. His associate John Ellis said of him that Bush had reached a dead end by age forty. This addiction may be a sign of the eruption of all the contradictions in the life of Bush junior: excessive dependency on his father in every matter, small or great, and taking vengeance on himself because of not achieving anything despite possessing wealth and prestige. Alcoholism was a way of escaping from problems that he could not confront in time. It was an escape that would recur whenever Bush confronted a difficult situation.

Religiosity
Bush has been trying for some time to harp on this note to win votes, to such an extent that one Zionist writer has almost made him into a saint. But there are some who are correctly classifying this sudden religiosity as a political game. Bush senior lost the presidential campaign against Clinton because he had no popularity in the interior states, where the conservative churches usually control elections. Accordingly, Bush played the role of the penitent who had repented of his sins, someone calling first on America to repent and then on the entire world to repent of unbelief (in the Trinity) and of immorality. It is a role that is receiving the full support of these churches, which have mobilized all their strength to back him. They, along with other forces (intelligence agencies, oil and arms lobbies) led to Bush's victory after putting pressure on the members of the court, which proclaimed his victory after he had lost the popular vote.

The truth is that Bush's religiosity contains great question marks, particularly since he boasts of his evil past, something that, as everybody knows, is incompatible with repentance.

Conclusion

The initial idea was to compare the leadership personalities of both the leader Sheikh Osama bin Laden and President Bush. However, after a small amount of study it became clear that the difference is enormous; indeed, there is no ground for comparison at all. One is abstemious, ascetic, pious, brave, honest, decent, and ready to give whatever is most precious in order to aid his religion and nation; the least that one can say about the other is that he is a sick man needing treatment.

I recalled the words of the poet:

Have you not seen that one lowers the sword's
worth when one says that it is sharper than a stick?

The article has therefore limited itself to mentioning Bush's unstable psychological background. The Europeans (France and Germany have well-established traditions of psychology) have read it and understand that the direction in which Bush is taking them is the abyss, and so their resistance to the American insanity has increased. Meanwhile, the Arab rulers have noticed nothing at all unusual. They are still competing to visit him and gain his approval. Birds of a feather flock together!

Even America's intellectuals have understood the situation well. Here is what an American writer said to Bush: "You have been a drunkard, a thief, an unpunished draft dodger, a cry-baby. . . . For the sake of all sacred and accepted values, resign from the presidency now and leave your family name some honor." [Editor's note: Michael Moore in his book *Stupid White Men*.]

CHAPTER 9
Toward a New Strategy in Resisting the Occupier

MUHAMMAD KHALIL AL-HAKAYMAH

Since al-Suri's capture in Pakistan, al-Hakaymah has emerged as both al Qaida's leading strategist and, some say, spymaster. In 1979, al-Hakaymah joined the terrorist group al-Gamaa al-Islamiya, the group that assassinated Anwar Sadat and is the most recent group to publicly declare its allegiance to al Qaida. Hakaymah was arrested after the Sadat assassination, but upon his release he returned to violent jihad. He has been arrested many times, reportedly once alongside Omar Abdul Rahman (the "blind sheikh"), who is currently in a U.S. prison for his part in the 1993 World Trade Center bombing.

In late 1980 Hakaymah went to Afghanistan to fight against the Soviets, and after the fall of the Soviet Union he spent some time in Britain. After 9/11 he fled Britain and is now reportedly in hiding along the Pakistan-Afghanistan border.

"Toward a New Strategy" marks his entry into the world of strategic thinking, but it has quickly gathered a wide readership within the jihadist community, which has been searching for ways to combat American initiative in the global war on terror. He recently released an analysis of the weaknesses of U.S. intelligence agencies (this will be included in a future volume of jihadist writings), which is expected to be part of a trilogy on how to combat America's antiterror forces.

Introduction

Today's wrathful Islamic *ummah* is in dire need of someone to guide it toward a new strategy to resist the Zionist-Crusader occupier, so as to make it a partner in the third world war. The jihad movement is the one authorized—and the only one—to whom this responsibility has been entrusted. Now that five years have past since the beginning of the Zionist-Crusader war, we must stop to examine the mechanisms for confronting the enemy. We must reflect on the path of the jihad and correct the mistakes of the battle so as to maintain our strategic goals and light the way before the youth of the *ummah*, whose active participation we hope for in the ongoing war with the greatest military power that human history has ever known.

What we shall say here is a private opinion about the movement and military matters, based on personal experiences, study, comparison, and conversations with experienced mujahideen leaders and cadres. Most of these topics are not questions of religious doctrine, but opinions based on the lessons of experience—matters of opinion, war, and strategy.

The purpose of these lines is to sketch a new strategy for the pitched battle that our *ummah* is fighting against an iniquitous enemy that hates Islam and its people. These lines are directives that we hope will be a military guide to every field commander, directing him to the correct way that will enable him to realize the hopes of our *ummah* that seeks decisive victory against its enemies—with the permission of God, who is mighty and exalted.

Preface

The Soviet Union once had an ideology and program. It was a military legend that the Western alliance could not eliminate. On the military level, the Soviet Union represented the greatest land power that history ever knew. As a civilization, it promoted the Communist theory, developed its theoretical framework, and made it into an ideology and religion that spread through half the world. The rulers of Muslims gave allegiance to it and subjected their peoples to it. The Communist outlook inflicted a great defeat on the liberal capitalist outlook, and the Western camp realized that only the tide of a cohesively wrought civilization could stop this Communist tide. Of course, they themselves were incapable of being the civilizational tide to confront communism. Since nothing was on the horizon except Islam, they had no choice but to urge their subaltern rulers to allow the return of jihad. Thus the gate was opened to the Islamists. The Soviet bear, for his part, was overhasty: he wanted the warm waters and oil of the Arabs. So the Soviet bear fell in Afghanistan, the Afghanistan of Islam and jihad. The jihad was led by religious scholars, and with them the heroic Afghan people, who sacrificed everything in order to be ruled by Islam. The experiment enjoyed worldwide Islamic renown: The flower of the *ummah* went to Afghanistan; Islam was victorious; the Soviet bear perished, and with him perished his theory and ideology. His regimes dissolved, along with everyone who sang his praise, save a few. Eastern Europe, most of the countries of Africa, and central Asia were liberated. Revolutions spread in them, and the Soviet Union became just a memory. The following question comes to mind: If the Soviet Union ruled half the world with its tremendous military machine and a well-organized theoretical outlook, what does the Western liberal-imperialist camp possess? The answer is: a tremendous military machine and an outlook of egoism and licentiousness more fragile than the Communist outlook. However much strength a military machine attains, it will never rule the world without having a real civilizational tide. One civilizational tide can only be eradicated by a stronger civilizational tide. Remember: The Mongols once possessed tremendous strength, but they were defeated in the face of the Muslim armies.

After the collapse of the Soviet Union, all of its satellites collapsed. There is no doubt—indeed, it is certain—that the collapse of the new Zionist-Crusader system will generate two things.

1. An unprecedented political vacuum. There will be more than one alternative, represented by the countries of the Old World that ruled the world in the past, and China or India might rise as poles dominating the policies of nations.

2. The breakup of the order subordinate to that system and the liberation of nations from the bonds of rulers, who will flee to their benefactors. That is the main point: we shall no more hear of the House of Saud and its sisters in the [Persian] Gulf or the other secular regimes. Who will inherit? Those who prepare well to meet the future: the Islamists, by God's will, however much their opinions and schools differ.

Therefore, victory in the coming battle against the Zionist-Crusader alliance is clear and evident, but it will be very taxing.

Fighting Tactics to Be Used

Warfare by Secret Groups with Unlinked, Impermanent Cells, to Be Used in Countries Directly Occupied by the Enemy
The believing mujahideen have proved that they are unequaled fighters on the fields of open confrontations. The unequal balance between them and their enemies has not stood as an obstacle to their victories in the face of regular armies.

The clearest examples of such victories in our experience are the first Afghan jihad, Bosnia, and Chechnya. This time, however, the enemy has adopted a new fighting strategy and a tactic unfamiliar to the mujahideen. It appeared in Afghanistan and Iraq and consisted of the following:

• Reliance on local collaborator forces carrying out the enemy's orders on the ground (the northerners in Afghanistan and the secular parties in Iraq).

• Reliance on isolating the target country from its neighborhood, neutralizing that neighborhood, or relying on it as a springboard offering logistical services to the enemy's forces (Pakistan and Iran).

• Reliance on overwhelming air and missile superiority to destroy every hostile target on the ground and in the area of the incident.

• Willingness to massacre civilians in order to realize military goals, disregarding all forms of public opinion.

• Bypassing the international community and all opposing opinion, bending them to its project by means of intimidation or neglect, now that America has really become the sole pole controlling the policies of countries and subjecting them to its interest.

• Turning the Islamic peoples into mere impotent onlookers of events, using the rulers and their agents as a means to keep these peoples out of the circle of conflict and action.

The result of these things was the destruction of the military positions of the Taliban in Afghanistan and the Kurdish positions of the Ansar al-Islam in northeastern Iraq. There was cooperation with the northern [Northern Alliance] forces led by [Gen. Muhammad] Fahim, which advanced into the areas from which the mujahideen withdrew in

Afghanistan—cooperation by means of heavy and concentrated aerial and rocket bombardment. In Iraq, the local Kurdish collaborator militias advanced to eliminate the remaining mujahideen on the ground. Those who escaped over the border into the neighboring country were taken prisoner under international agreements and conspiracies.

In addition, the enemy adopted the method of security hunts, by means of which it liquidated secret jihadist organizations and other cells in many places in cooperation with the local security apparatus. This has happened in Saudi Arabia, Morocco, Indonesia, and some countries of East Asia.

Thus the present strategy has now become unproductive and unsuited to the fighting strategy with which the enemy is confronting us. It has become necessary to look for an alternative: namely, the method of warfare by secret groups with unlinked cells not permanent in the same area and with many multiple cells. The features of an example of this are clearly evident in the operations of the Iraqi resistance. This tactic is useful for countries directly occupied by the enemy.

Individual Jihad, to Be Used in Countries Not Directly Occupied

This school of jihad is very old. An instance of this method is what happened late in the life of the Prophet, when al-Aswad al-'Ansi apostatized in Yemen, seized power there, and overwhelmed the Muslims. A man whom the Prophet described as "blessed" took charge of handling the matter. He acted of his own accord as an individual, assassinated al-Aswad al-'Ansi, and turned the balance so that Islam took firm root in Yemen. The angel Gabriel announced the glad tidings of the decisive victory by a handful of individual mujahideen to the Prophet.

This kind of individual jihad has recurred throughout Islamic history. In the time of the Crusades, when rulers were corrupt and the nation decadent, groups of mujahideen responded to the crisis. Many isolated expeditions and groups carried out the obligation of jihad. In modern Arab history there was the famous incident when a mujahid by himself was able to turn the balance of forces and influence the course of a major colonial campaign. It took place when the mujahid Sulayman al-Halabi, may God have mercy on him, fled from Aleppo, my venerable city in northwestern Syria, to Jerusalem. There he asked one of the *ulema* for a fatwa to kill Kléber, the commander of the French expedition, whom Napoleon Bonaparte had appointed as his deputy over Egypt. Al-Halabi managed to reach Kléber and kill him, and this was one of the reasons for the French expedition's departure from Egypt. The only price for this was that Sulayman al-Halabi and the sheikh who gave him the fatwa won martyrdom in the way of God, since they were executed.

Since the second Gulf War (Desert Storm) in 1990 and the rise of the New World Order, this school has revived. Dozens of individual operations have taken place since then in various locations of the Arab and Islamic world, and they continue to the present day.

In the United States, Sayyid Nusayr killed the Zionist bigot, Rabbi Meir Kahana. One of the Jews most strongly against Muslims in Palestine, Kahana had a program to expel the Palestinians completely from Palestine. Kahana's murder led to his group's dissolution and extinction.

In Jordan, a Jordanian conscript from the border patrol opened fire, killing a number of Jewish student girls who were making gestures mocking Muslim prayers.

In Egypt, the heroic soldier Salman Khatir opened fire on his own decision on a number of Jews on the Egyptian-Israeli border.

On the border of Jordan with Israel, dozens of border-crossing operations have been carried out by young mujahideen—some of them carrying only a kitchen knife!—to attack Jewish patrols on the west bank of the Jordan River.

In Beirut, a mujahid went up to the roof of an apartment building and launched several RBJ rockets at the Russian embassy during one of the Russian campaigns against the Chechens.

During the days of the Gulf War, an old Moroccan stabbed a dozen French tourists in Morocco.

In the Emirates, the body of an Italian was discovered.

A young man stabbed a number of foreigners in Amman, Jordan, and opened fire on them.

In Palestine, many individual actions are being carried out by citizens revolting against settlers or soldiers of the occupation.

In Pakistan, mujahideen have killed a number of Americans and Jews.

In Egypt, a citizen presented Hosni Mubarak with a letter and then stabbed him with a knife—the guards killed him.

In Jordan, a group of four individuals formed a cell to assassinate collaborators. They were able to execute a number of them.

In Egypt, two veiled girls opened fire on a bus of Jewish tourists in the heart of Cairo.

Individual jihad using the method of urban or rural guerrilla warfare is the foundation for sapping the enemy and bringing him to a state of collapse and withdrawal. It will pave the way for the desired strategic goal.

What mandates these methods as a strategic opinion is the imbalance of forces between the resistance and the large invading alliance of unbelievers, apostates, and hypocrites. Some of the factors are:

1. The failure of the method of action by pyramidal organizations in view of the international security assault and regional and international coordination: A modus operandi must be developed whose cells these security agencies cannot manage to abort by arresting their members on the basis of torture and confessions.
2. The inability of secret organizations to absorb all the young men of the *ummah* who want to perform the duty of jihad and resistance by some action without being forced to commit to the consequences of joining a central organization.
3. The extensiveness of the enemy presence, the variety of his goals, and his presence in many locations makes it difficult for fighting fronts to arise, just as it makes it difficult for central organizations to be established.
4. The collapse of the idea of permanent, open fronts and confrontation with the enemy due to the enemy's use of the strategy of air resolution by destructive rocket bombardment and satellite directed air projectiles. This is a fact that must be recognized, and planning for confrontation must be done on its basis.

Means to Be Used in Fighting

In the past five years, the jihad movement has created fighting means that not every member of the *ummah* can adopt due to their great technical complexity and sizable material requirements. Also, the jihad movement unintentionally reinforced the idea that there could be no fighting except by martyrdom operations and car bombs. The result of this was to prevent the *ummah* from participating in the existential battle we are fighting against the enemy. It therefore has become necessary to find and implement simpler or less costly means, means that it is easy to obtain and master everywhere, so that we can motivate the sons of the *ummah* to participate with us in today's battle through the tactic of individual jihad. Otherwise, the *ummah* will continue to play the role of the spectator or onlooker throughout this possibly lengthy period of battle.

We do not mean to call for abandoning the use of martyrdom missions or car bombs. Not at all! The results that the battle in Iraq has manifested by using these means have been stunning. Martyrdom operations and explosive charges have been the weapons that have kept the enemy sleepless. They remain the only weapons distinguishing the mujahideen in the battle and that the enemy will never possess.

Martyrdom operations and explosive charges can be weapons to deter the enemy in countries directly occupied by the enemy, with the *ummah* present in the field to back the mujahideen and support them by all material and moral means, such as Iraq, Afghanistan, Palestine, Chechnya, and Kashmir.

However, in countries where certain targets important to the enemy are located and where we want continued resistance against the enemy with the participation of the *ummah*, means must be found that are accessible to the members of the *ummah*.

If we consider our contemporary history, we find that the British, French, and Italian occupation left the Muslim lands in defeat without the mujahideen's using martyrdom operations or car bombs. They left because they encountered continued resistance every day and everywhere from the young men of the *ummah*.

Furthermore, the tyrant governments in all cases after every big martyrdom operation proceed to eradicate all the organized groups engaged in jihad in the country, so as to find those responsible for the operation. They do this even if it requires inflicting collective punishment on all the inhabitants of the area, as happened in Sinai after the operations to kill Jews at Sharm al-Sheikh and Dahab. In this way the battle usually changes from fighting the enemy into fighting with the regime, and this will divert us from the primary strategic goal, which is to eject the occupying assailant.

Whoever thinks about the theory of fighting the enemy in Muslim lands not directly occupied by the enemy will find that we fight them there for the sake of incidents to cause political pressure and psychological collapse, so that they leave our lands. It is not a fight to eradicate them. This being the case, realism and self-interest support the idea that carrying out a small operation every month against the enemy will have more of an impact on him than a big operation every year or two.

There are many simple and easy means of jihad that every field commander should implement generally and teach to individuals in the jihad against the personnel of the occupying enemy.

Military Targets

The targets that the mujahideen must keep in mind are those that will effectively weaken the Crusader-Zionist campaign against the lands of Islam. One must not become preoccupied with targets with no impact. One must not be hasty in selecting the target with an impact.

An important note to which attention needs to be drawn: The division of people into military and civilian is not part of Islamic law. Islamic law divides people into combatants and noncombatants. A combatant by the standard of Islamic law is anyone who himself fights or who helps the combat by his wealth or opinion.

On that basis, the peoples of the Crusader West by the criterion of Islamic law are combatant peoples fighting the Muslims—for the following reasons:

1. Because these peoples have chosen their rulers and parliaments by their own free will. In other words, they have chosen the executive authority that is practicing aggression against Islam and Muslims. They have also chosen the legislative authority that oversees and calls the executive to account and that approves or rejects its policies at will.

2. Because these peoples pay taxes to fund campaigns of aggression against Muslims.

3. Because they supply men, funds, and expertise to the armies attacking Islamic lands.

4. Because they supply men, talents, and information to the Crusader security agencies that seek to harm Muslims. Even opponents of the policies of the Crusader governments in these nations pay taxes, provide information, and participate in the fight against Islam and its people.

Furthermore, all the political parties in the Crusader West supported the establishment of Israel and its rape of the Palestinians, and they still support Israel's survival and existence to this day; indeed, they support it with money, weapons, knowledge, and men.

Important Directives for Field Commanders

Taking Care Not to Kill Muslims by Mistake

Mujahideen must carefully think out the consequences of every operation according to Islamic law. They must also carefully think out the operation militarily and in terms of security. One of the most important aspects of what we are discussing is the question of any Muslims who will be killed by bombings carried out by the mujahideen. One must systematically avoid killing them by every means. One must calculate the yield and importance of the operation and the balance between Muslims unintentionally hit by error and the expected harm and impact on unbelievers. In some operations we have seen bombs intended to kill a few members of a military patrol of unbelievers placed in a market crowded with Muslims; or we have seen a car bomb at the gate of an American consulate, outside the wall fencing off the garden, behind which are located offices where most of the people are not Americans. No rational person would consider it probable that a single American would be hit in such an operation! Only a few of the enemies targeted are killed or wounded, perhaps even none, while dozens of Muslims, including children, women, and innocent people, suffer death, wounding, and destruction of property. It is a result known to any rational person by a simple accounting and study of the place and the probable presence of Muslims in it.

There is a big difference that needs to be kept in mind between the use of explosives in unbelievers' countries and capitals, such as Tel Aviv, Washington, and London, and their use in Muslims' capitals and lands.

Striking the wrongdoer and unbeliever does not justify not being careful about Muslim. Does the likelihood of killing a few of the unbelievers' stooges or aides, men who have no value and who change nothing in the course of the long-term battle we are fighting, justify the certain or probable death of dozens of believing souls? I do not think that such a purpose or intention justifies such an action in any such cases.

Many texts from the Qur'an and the Prophet stress the sanctity of the Muslim soul. Let those who strive in the way of God ponder these texts and be careful in their actions.

Some mujahideen may think that the mere intention to target unbelievers for death and not any Muslims who might die is sufficient to permit them to carry out such actions. I think that a sound intention and purpose by itself is not enough; God only accepts from His servant what is done sincerely for His sake and is correct. Correctness means following the Qur'an and the Sunnah as scholars have expounded it. Part of this, without doubt, is to avoid spilling in battle the blood of believers and of those who are legally protected, to the extent that one can.

If the target that the mujahideen aim at will produce such certain harm to the enemy (according to the predominant opinion among experts in the battle) as shall contribute to an enemy defeat and Muslim victory, as when the target is an important enemy leader or inflicts effective, heavy loss in the unbelievers' ranks; and if the mujahideen do all in their power to keep Muslims away from the scene of the incident, spare them, and select a time when few of them are present, taking every possible precaution; if, after they have made every effort, fate causes some Muslims to be hit in spite of precautions—then I hope that God will forgive them because of their having done all they could and because of the soundness of their intention and purpose.

While discussing this relevant question, we have heard things from some mujahideen that suggest that they are unconcerned about losses that occur among ordinary Muslims. For example, some say that most of the Muslims hit were wrongdoers, were cooperating with the occupation, or were heretics with many corrupt beliefs and with other attributes, whether true or false. Such arguments, however, are false. The basic principle regarding them is that their Islam renders them protected and requires that they be spared. No reputable scholar holds the position that their lives may be taken. Yet I have seen on occasion that the psychological state that some mujahideen reach because of pressure from God's enemies on the one hand, the reluctance of ordinary people to come to the aid of God's religion on the other hand, and the corruption surrounding them, has caused some of them to treat the question of real caution lightly. This is a serious matter to which attention must be paid in the future.

Avoiding Cruel Methods of Fighting, Expect for Necessity

The jihad movement must avoid any behavior that the masses who love us do not understand or approve, so long as such avoidance does not involve a clear violation of Islamic law and as long as there are other options that can be used. In other words, we must not throw the masses, ignorant as they are, into the sea before we teach them how to swim. Someone may ask why we shouldn't cast fear into the hearts of the Crusaders and their aides. Isn't bringing villages and cities down on the heads of their inhabitants crueler than beheading? Aren't seven-ton cluster bombs and depleted uranium bombs more loathsome than beheading? Isn't murder by torture in Abu Ghraib and Bagram worse than beheading? Isn't violating the honor of men and women more painful and more far-reaching in effect than beheading?

You may ask all these questions and more, and you have the right to do so. But it will not change the reality of the battle at all. The public opinion supporting us will not understand it. This public opinion is being subjected to a vicious campaign of disinformation by the huge media of lies and deceptions. We of all people least need to raise questions about the value of our operations in the minds, hearts, and intellects of Muslim public opinion sympathetic with us.

We are in a battle. More than half of the battle is taking place in the forum of the media. In the media battle we are in a race for the hearts and minds of our *ummah*. However great our resources may be, they will never equal one-thousandth of the media resources of the Great Satan's kingdom making war on us. We can kill prisoners with bullets and achieve what we want without bringing questions on ourselves or having to respond to doubts about scenes of beheadings.

Concern for the Role of the *Ulema*

Every field commander must show concern for the *ulema* by not publicizing disputes that lay Muslims might not understand and by being fair to people. Sometimes a scholar may hold an innovation or fall short in some way that does not render him an unbeliever. He may even show dedication to jihad, fighting, and giving of oneself in the way of God. History has celebrated the positions of Ash'ari and Maturidi scholars in times of jihad and defense of Muslim sanctities.

Because the public considers the *ulema* to be the symbol and badge of Islam, disparaging them could lead to public disdain for religion and the clergy. It could encourage atheists and secularists to belittle everything Islamic. This will cause more harm than the benefit to be gained by criticizing a scholar for an innovation that does not constitute unbelief or for a legal position.

Naturally, what we are saying has nothing to do with collaborating *ulema*—traitors and hypocrites who have allied with the Crusaders and Jews.

As for the *ulema* who are active and who strive in jihad, if they hold some innovation or error that does not constitute unbelief, we must find some means of dealing with it—some way to absorb and benefit from their ability.

Concern for Unity of Goal

The overall goal of the mujahideen, after the occupier's departure, is the establishment of an Islamic emirate that shall be a point of departure for defending Islam and Muslims and a step toward reviving the caliphate. In Iraq we must not forget that Jerusalem is a stone's throw from Baghdad. If the Islamic emirate arises in Iraq with God's help and is able to penetrate the traitorous Jordanian entity so as to stand on the borders of Palestine, and if, with God's permission, the mujahideen inside and outside Palestine link up, then there shall take place the greatest victory and ultimate triumph, God willing.

One of the main elements of success in our battle is not to lose sight of our strategic goals. They must always remain present before us. We must not deviate from the overall line by a policy of reaction to what we might receive at the hands of tyrant regimes. This is the wisdom of a lifetime's experience that we are offering to the field leadership. We have seen a great deal of reactive policy at the level of individuals and leaders, and we have often seen attempts to return to the original course and strategic goal.

Part of our strategy is to maintain unity of goal and not become involved in side battles that divert us from achieving our strategic goal. Every field commander must counsel his mujahideen to be patient in the face of provocations coming from the security agencies in his country. One of the most dangerous influences on the leadership in this area is the zeal of supporters, especially enthusiastic young men burning to come to the aid of the faith. Such zeal must be moderated by wisdom.

It is self-evident that anyone busy fighting the Americans must be especially concerned with minimizing the number of his enemies and maximizing the number of his friends. How could this be otherwise, when one is facing the world's strongest force?

Concern for Popular Support

The Muslim *ummah* is in a state of foment due to external attack and internal misery. The militant vanguard of the *ummah* must make proper use of this state of foment to turn the power of the angry *ummah* into an active, effective movement of change that brings the *ummah* to victory, God permitting.

If after liberating our country from the occupier, the mujahideen seek to establish an Islamic emirate according to the prophetic model, this goal will not be realized by the jihad movement while it is cut off from popular support. Even if the jihad movement takes the road of a surprise military coup, such a coup will take place only with a minimum amount of popular support that will be the element separating victory from defeat. In the absence of such popular support, the jihad movement will be crushed in the darkness, far from the masses who are preoccupied with feeding their children. The conflict between the jihadist elite and the arrogant authorities will be restricted to the cellars of prisons, far from publicity and the light, which is exactly what the secularist forces dominating our country want. These forces have no hope of annihilating the jihad movement, but they are making a concerted effort to isolate it from the misled or fearful Muslim masses. So our planning must try to incorporate the Muslim masses into the battle and into leadership of the mass jihad movement and not fight the battle far from the masses.

The Muslim masses, for many reasons that this is not the time to rehearse, are aroused only by a foreign occupying enemy, especially if this enemy is primarily Jewish and secondarily American. This is the reason for the popular support that the mujahideen enjoy in Iraq, Palestine, and Afghanistan.

The desired emirate based on Islamic law demands political work alongside the fighting and war, political work whose nucleus will be the mujahideen, around whom will gather the tribes and their sheikhs, the leading figures, scholars, businessmen, opinion shapers, and all people of distinction not soiled by fawning on the occupation and well disposed toward the defenders of Islam.

We must understand the dimensions of the conflict between truth and falsehood. We must be aware of the balances of force and legitimate alliances and the strategy of neutralization and confrontation.

When we study our situation, we must not neglect to become acquainted with the strength of our enemy and find out who is on our side, who against us, and who is standing neutral in the calculations of war, watching and waiting to follow whoever prevails.

The world is looking for change in the light of forces that support it, and it sees no success without these forces. Therefore the *ummah* has relied sometimes on the East and at other times on the West. When matters inclined to the latter, the *ummah* inclined totally toward it.

Today, the whole world is allied against us. Anyone who opposes this alliance is not doing so out of love for us but out of desire to increase his share of the spoils (we being the spoils). We desire a sincere ally, one who will make sacrifices for us and not betray us. Such an ally, in brief, are our Islamic peoples.

Because this conflict is a long-term one that could extend for a generation or more, it is wrong to engage in it in isolation from the *ummah* or as its proxy. Rather, the jihad current represents the vanguard of this blessed *ummah*.

Nations that do not rely on this world and do not stint of their money, blood, and sons are strong nations able to cause the desired change. All they lack is wise leadership, a clear vision to follow, and weapons in their hands to protect their course and crush their foe. For all these reasons, we stress the need for political action to proceed in parallel with military action, with the alliance, cooperation, and alignment of all who influence and shape opinion in the field. We cannot lay down a particular method of political action. Every commander knows best about the conditions in his field. We must take care that you have around you circles of popular support, assistance, and cooperation. We repeat our warning—and it is a strong warning—against separating from the masses.

CHAPTER 10

The Call to Global Islamic Resistance

AL-SURI

Editor's Note: This is an extract from a 1,600-page manifesto. As this entire document is critical to understanding today's jihad movement, a separate book is being published to reduce the original to a more manageable size (*A Terrorist's Call to Global Jihad*, Naval Institute Press, 2008). This extract is offered to present the reader with the current state of the jihad movement from an insider's perspective.

Abu Musab al-Suri (a.k.a. Mustafa Setmariam Nasar and Omar Abdel Hakim) was born in October 1958 in Aleppo, Syria. Nasar was a member of the radical Syrian Muslim Brotherhood and was forced to seek exile from his homeland during the 1980s, traveling throughout the Middle East and North Africa and eventually finding his way to the ongoing jihad in Afghanistan.

Until his capture in Pakistan in 2006, al-Suri was al Qaida's foremost strategic thinker. He has written several books on different aspects of the jihadist movement, released dozens of tapes, and taught many classes that detail practical methods of conducting jihad against the West. In addition to his writing efforts, he is also believed to have been one of the chief planners behind the July 2005 London bombings and the 2004 Madrid train bombings.

Though born in Syria, he lived in the West for many years and worked in both Britain and Spain before returning to Afghanistan to join al Qaida and open up his own training camp for incoming jihadists. The Call to Global Islamic Resistance *is his master work and was released just before his capture. In it he gives a history of the jihad movement from its inception, details its current condition, and lays out a detailed plan for carrying the jihad forward in the twenty-first century. This work has gained a reputation as the* Mein Kampf *(Hitler) or* What Is to Be Done? *(Lenin) of the jihad movement.*

At the onset of the twenty-first century, the Islamic *ummah* is enduring American-Zionist, Crusader-Western invasions, helped by the cooperation of hypocritical governments that control the Arab and Islamic world.

Many jihadist cadres have been destroyed, and a large number of their bases have vanished due to military attacks conducted by this alliance of infidels and hypocritical Arab and Islamic governments. This has placed the continuity of the jihadist movement—and its ability to preserve its purity under threat.

Likewise, the Islamic awakening is enduring an intellectual decline due to the efforts of hypocrites among the *ulema* and the defeatists within its leadership. This decline threatens both the core group and the Awakening's masses, just as it also threatens the creed, identity, and existence of the *ummah*.

The American war of ideas and the attack on our educational system began in the first decade of the twentieth century. The continuation of this assault on the foundational principles of the *ummah* may eventually lead to the *ummah*'s destruction. There is a need to preserve the religious, intellectual, and cultural identity of the *ummah* and sustain the thoughts of the Islamic Awakening and particularly its jihadist vanguard.

I believe that, due to these circumstances, jihadist nuclei will be strewn about with no common ideology or identity to unite them—except the goal of repelling the crusader assault.

It is possible that our enemies will note the disarray arising from these disparate centers of Muslim resistance and will exploit these mistakes to cripple the jihad and drive a wedge between the jihad's resistance and its audience within the *ummah*, thereby forcing the jihad along the path of dispersion and defeat.

Because of the continuous fall of martyrs from the leadership and the destruction of cadres, which had been prepared methodologically over a long period of time, the majority of our current resistance and jihadist groups lack an educational, political, legal, and intellectual paradigm that can serve as a reference for them. They have no means to properly prepare new cadres or a fixed foundation to help settle their disputes.

The modern Crusader-Jewish, American-led campaign against the Arab and Islamic world has clearly announced its goals: total elimination of the civilizational, religious, political, economic, social, and cultural existence of Muslims. The Bush administration has announced its plans for the next decade:

1. Transforming the political map of the Middle East and the Arab-Islamic world, that is, transforming the ruling systems and reconstructing, replacing, or forming them anew.
2. Redrawing the map of certain countries, encouraging fractiousness as well as localized, religious, ethnic, and political strife.
3. Destroying cultural and identity-based resistance movements and reconstituting the social fabric by removing the religious, intellectual, and moral foundation of the region and reshaping this foundation on the basis of Western thought, specifically American-Zionist thought.
4. Hegemony over the sources of wealth in the region, particularly oil and gas, mineral resources, and other agricultural and livestock resources, so as to pump them through the arteries of the invaders and the Zionist entity implanted in the heart of the region.
5. Transforming the region into a market for liquidating imperialist products via so-called partnership and free trade agreements in the Middle East.

Numerous media sources have revealed that America with Britain and Israel behind her (along with all of the NATO and European nations rotating in America's orbit) has sought to use all its military, strategic, economic, media might to realize these objectives.

In short, the world is witnessing Western civilization's most insolent, malevolent, barbaric attack in history. The West is following the leadership of a gang of Crusader, would-be Zionists in the American administration. However, it is also known that this "Third Crusader Campaign" is a malicious continuation of the two campaigns that preceded it—the first during the eleventh and twelfth Christian centuries, and the second, which spanned from the seventeenth century until the middle of the twentieth century.

We stand before a military invasion armed with the newest military instruments and scientific technology, supporting the most destructive strategic plans. They use tanks to implement programs for social, religious, and cultural transformation, for replacing the Islamic faith, and fragmenting the Arab and Muslim identity. They plan programs for reshaping our societies, including intellectual and cultural elements, educational changes, and media programs, which they hope will reshape everything, including the Friday sermon on the pulpits of Muslim mosques.

In short, the hole has grown wider than the patch, and we need to step back and contemplate the methods we can use to confront this campaign. These methods must be much more than empty, superficial, or spastic reactions. We are facing an overwhelming disaster, which is reaching its tragic apex. We must understand that for the first time in Muslim history, and possibly the history of all colonized people resisting invasion, that the colonizer has focused his attack, using all of the instruments of power on the gigantic fifth column planted within Arab and Islamic societies.

The American attack today depends—and we must accept this agonizing reality—on complete cooperation from the overwhelming majority of the current Arab rulers. These rulers, because they think this is how they can best defend their own interests, cooperate with the plans of the American colonizers. They follow American leadership and make war against the religion of the people and against the jihadists. What's more, these rulers have mobilized all of their security, media, and controlling apparatuses to annihilate all seeds of resistance to the American invasion. This begins with the suppression of any form of association established for nonviolent change, demonstration, or opposition and ends with the killing, imprisonment, and banishment of anyone who argues for the formation of resistance groups, especially the seeds of armed and legitimate jihad.

If only the calamity ended with the ruling systems' alliances with the invading enemy. However, the calamity is much worse because considerable segments of Arab and Islamic societies have been transformed intellectually, culturally, and politically so as they are also willing to assist the occupiers. This is the case even if some of these societal elements are part of the opposition to the apostate ruling systems. In places like Iraq and Afghanistan, opposition movements present themselves as even more prepared than the current ruling systems to serve the American cause.

At the hands of our countrymen, who have names like our own, who wear our clothes and speak our tongue, services are offered to the colonizer to assassinate her *ummah*, defeat her religion, kill her sons, and wipe out all elements of civilization. These collaborating groups are not confined to intellectual movements, nor to specific ethnic or religious groups. Within this vile column are those who claim a variety of identities, beginning with so-called Islam and continuing with every color of secularist and political demon in our lands.

It is a disaster that many of the good Islamic *ulema*, as well as party and organization leaders, have begun to sell the notion of prostration and our inability to wage war. The enemy media has convinced them to sell the idea of peaceful coexistence, intercivilizational exchange, peaceful dialogue, and mutual understanding with colonizers, who devastate us day and night with smart bombs and rockets, and who destroys us with armies comprised of our stupid sons. All this is proclaimed under the pretense of moderation, or wisdom.

Thus are God's religion and its clear commands abandoned. It is commanded that we wage jihad against this assault and we fight the enemies of God with all available means, and all of the strength we can muster, and resisting them until the last spark of life. But the battle cries of the noble ones are suppressed. Muslim demonstrations are beaten down under the batons and tear gas canisters of the Fear Forces—otherwise known as the "Security Forces." They are crushed under most vile fatwas presented by the sultan's battle-shirking *ulema*, who are the missionaries of prostration, shame, and destitution.

Nothing now remains in the field resisting the Crusaders apart from a few pure hearts and here and there weak brigand cells who are bleeding martyrs, most often for no gain. If conditions remain as described above, there is no doubt that we are threatened.

I do not mean that we are threatened with extinction, as God proclaimed for his *ummah* longevity, triumph, and victory. But we are threatened with conquest, hardship, and pain. We are faced with hunger, fear, killing, humiliation, and destitution. It is, therefore, necessary that a jihad-waging group of noble elite step forward and present methods for arousing resistance and to awaken the *ummah* to join the fight against the enemies of God.

Axes of the Resistance

I believe—and this consideration would be obvious to anyone—that the size of the elite resisting the invading enemies is a frighteningly small segment of the *ummah*. This is not only due to the viciousness of the enemy attack, but also because of the decadence, and the individual acceptance of colonialism and defeat within the *ummah*.

I believe that in order to engage in this long-lasting war it is necessary to devise a multifaceted program that will give birth to the seeds of the resistance in the *ummah*.

In the end, successful jihad will only happen within an *ummah* in which the fighting creed is firmly established and clarified. This must happen in order to attain the "Revolutionary Jihadist Climate" that will spontaneously give rise to instruments of resistance. I think that the problem of creating this climate is too great to for just the shoulders of the jihadist elite alone, especially since this elite faces near extinction due to global struggle against terrorism that America is leading. Through America's exploitation of the events of September 2001, this assault has gone beyond the destruction of numerous cadres and jihadist groups around the world. It has also destroyed part of the Islamic Awakening that has supported the jihad. With that in mind, I believe it is the obligation of the believing elite to work toward three aims:

The Religious-Cultural Aim: Set in place programs for preserving religious identity and preserving the pure defining intellectual, cultural, and social elements of the Arab and Islamic people.

The Political-Intellectual Aim: Set in place programs for stimulating political activism, local organizations, and civil society organizations as well as encouraging peaceful media activities that nourish the intellectual and cultural existence of the Arab and Islamic *ummah*.

The Military Aim: Set in place programs and methods for training in the fighting jihadist creed and for preparation in its educational and spiritual facets. Also setting up programs for training in the essential military sciences, so as to enable the immediate implementation of a "Global Islamic Resistance" that will confront America within our Arab and Islamic lands and then in her homeland.

1. Military work and armed jihadist action are the things that will compel the enemy into retreat and lead this *ummah* to victory.

Without military resistance, the influence of all peaceful work—however important will be scattered to the winds. As long as the infidel-Zionist-Crusader–invading colonizer is perched on our chests and in our lands, the entire *ummah* will remain guilty and responsible before God for not sufficiently repelling the enemy.

Violent jihad is as an individual duty obligatory upon every Muslim. All the *ulema* have said this, and it becomes even more pressing now that the attacker has entered our abode.

2. Armed jihad does not arise from a vacuum and will not transform into the desired magnitude until a revolutionary jihadist climate exists to give rise to it. This means we must invest great effort into a variety of nonfighting fields—proselytizing, media, education, and defining elements of our religion. It also means broadcasting the Islamic creed and the laws of the sharia, which will fill the heart of the believer with assuredness that militancy is a sharia obligation.

3. Political movement awareness constitutes—along with the religious conviction—the necessary foundations in the mind of the individual Muslim for moving into active fighting.

4. Fearlessness in jihad and armed action in the confrontation with America and her allies is undertaken by only a small percentage of the *ummah* that possesses resoluteness, conviction, and desire compelling it to direct action. Whereas there is a large part of the *ummah* that is convinced of the need for confrontation, its resoluteness on this matter has yet to reach the point of being classed as the highest Islamic obligation.

5. If the elite does not undertake the work of thwarting the enemies' programs for destroying our civilizational structure, then they will become extinct at the hands of the enemy's military effort. The *ummah* will not produce a replacement but will melt away under the enemy's media and educational barrage.

6. Preserving the religion and the defining elements of our civilization requires a plan of action that forces adherents to conduct clandestine dissemination and education. This kind of positive educational work multiplies the seeds of the resistance and provides the fuel of the revolution. Mosques and religious schools must play a large role in this area, just as religious education and study circles in people's homes play an important role. There is also an important role for women and female missionaries inside the family and the home to ensure that the younger generations adhere to their faith and culture.

7. Those employed in the political, media, intellectual, and cultural fields are able to disseminate the idea of civil resistance and its justifications. They are also able to defend our jihad both inside and outside of the country. Likewise, writing, protesting, and other works of civil resistance are works that are permissible under the "false democracy" of colonialism, and this can be used by our supporters safe from penalty or accusations of terrorism.

There are two very important observations concerning the field of non-violent civil resistance, whether in religious, political, or intellectual work:

First: It is never permissible, and is illegal according to the sharia, to join the governing apparatus under the pretext of "peaceful resistance" and service to the faith. Employment in any governing, parliamentary, executive, or judicial apparatuses is impermissible.

Second: It is never permissible for an individual working in the civil resistance and the political and media mission to commit the crime of slander against the jihad, the mujahideen, and the Muslim resistance fighters under the pretext of deflecting suspicion away from himself so as to continue his work.

This is because the object of his existence and the justification for his work is the creation of a climate for jihad and support for the resistance. How will resistance be born and continue if the most prominent Islamic missionaries, intellectuals, leaders, and literati within the *ummah* take it upon themselves to slander the jihad and the mujahideen and destroy the good reputation of the resistance and the resistance fighters?

At this moment, the jihadist media should avoid slandering those working in the field and, moreover, avoid accusing them of shirking battle and of lacking jihadist spirit—even if this were true of the bulk of them.

The Effect of 9/11 on the Jihadist Movement in Afghanistan

The Americans began their aggression by launching a series of air strikes that lasted from October 10 to November 11. For the ground offensive, the Americans relied on the Northern Alliance, which engaged in combat on three fronts. From the north, they advanced toward Kabul. From the southeast on the Pakistan border, they moved toward Kandahar. Lastly, from the northeast, they advanced towards Jalalabad.

The Northern Alliance are a bunch of thieves and criminals. Some of the tribes in the Northern Alliance support the American program, and the Americans helped them capture the cities one by one. The Taliban were besieged and subsequently surrendered to the Americans and their allies. One week after the fall of Kabul, they declared that the Taliban had been defeated and [Hamid] Karzai assumed power. The Americans ground forces gained control of Afghanistan and began implementing their ugly and dirty program by spending millions of dollars.

Subsequently, the Americans, under the leadership of Bush, declared a war against international terrorism. Pakistan aided the United States in the killing and imprisonment of the mujahideen who were inside its territory. In addition to America's main allies, the governments in the Arab and Islamic world participated in the war against terrorism. This state of affairs led to the complete destruction of the jihadist movement. The Arab mujahideen and immigrants faced the worst genocide in their history. This was the fate that Allah had in store for them. From 2001 to the writing of this text [September 2004], their losses included the following:

- The martyrdom of about 400 Arab mujahideen during the defense of Afghanistan. They faced serious losses on all fronts and many of them were killed in the intensive bombing campaign. Some of them fled to Pakistan. The government of Pakistan captured 150 mujahideen because of tribal treachery.
- In 2002, some of the mujahideen fled Tora Bora and were captured by Pakistani forces. Subsequently, they were handed over to the Americans.
- These prisoners were transferred to the Guantanamo Bay detention facility. This detention camp has a very bad reputation.
- From 2002 to September 2004, nearly 100 mujahideen were martyred in different battles with the Pakistani army, especially in the border regions and on different travel routes.
- Some Arab Afghans had fled with their families to Pakistan. The Pakistani government captured some 600 mujahideen from the latter group and handed them over to the American government. Some were sent to Guantanamo while others were imprisoned in Afghanistan.
- Iran captured more than 400 Arab mujahideen and handed them over to their respective countries. Iran admitted this action openly. There are still some 100 prisoners in Iran at the moment. The Iranians

are negotiating with the U.S. government concerning the fate of these prisoners.

From among 1,900 Arab mujahideen in Afghanistan, roughly 1,600 have been captured or killed. In all, nearly 75 percent of all Arab Afghans have either been captured or killed. This was accomplished through cooperation with the intelligence services of Europe and the Islamic world. Many friends or relatives of jihadists were also arrested and imprisoned, even though they had no connection with jihadist organizations or groups. The mujahideen of central Asia, especially the Uzbeks, also suffered tremendously in this war. Many of them were either killed or captured. Roughly 500 Uzbek mujahideen were martyred, not counting those who were captured. Many were killed in Waziristan by Pakistani forces, which were supported by the American military.

Many of the East Turkistan mujahideen faced a similar fate to their Uzbek brothers. The emir of the East Turkistan group was martyred along with some of his supporters. His name was Hasan Abu Muhammad al-Turkistani. He was pursued and killed by the Pakistani army (may Allah strike them down).

In mid-2003, Defense Minister [sic] Rumsfeld declared that the American military had killed or captured more than 3,000 terrorists. I believe this figure is accurate. Roughly half of them had been killed in Afghanistan, Pakistan, and Iran. According to official British statistics, nearly 300 terrorists and their supporters had been arrested and detained. Over a dozen other jihadists have been captured throughout Europe. Among Arab countries, Yemen carried out a huge campaign against jihadists and Arab Afghans as well as their supporters. The government killed or captured hundreds of them. Saudi Arabia also carried out a campaign against jihadist groups, who were accused of having ties to al Qaida. The Saudi government captured 220 mujahideen. They imprisoned and interrogated thousands of mujahideen. The reason behind the Saudi and Yemeni campaigns had to do with the fact that the largest group of Arab mujahideen had come from these two Arab states. The last major campaign took place in November 2003 in Morocco. The government of Morocco arrested hundreds of mujahideen and their supporters. Subsequently, many were executed while others were imprisoned for life. Still others received long prison sentences.

Throughout the globe, many mujahideen and their supporters were accused of committing terrorist acts. The war on terrorism stretched from the horn of Africa to the Philippines, Indonesia, and Southeast Asia. The American counterattack clearly was waged across the entire globe.

This unprecedented disaster came about for three main reasons:

1. The figure of 3,000 to 4,000 jihadists killed or captured is in fact a low estimation. The real numbers are much larger than that. The majority of the mujahideen living in Afghanistan had been killed or captured. This was also the case for the mujahideen who were residing in the Arab and Islamic world as well as in the West. The jihadist movement was uprooted and decimated.

2. The strike on the Arab mujahideen in central Asia, Afghanistan, and Pakistan killed off most of the senior members of the jihadist organizations and the first generation of Arab Afghans. By 2000, only about 150 of these mujahideen had survived the onslaught. The flower of the jihadist movement was killed or captured. Only a fraction of the mujahideen survived or were not captured.

3. The American attack decimated the senior leadership of those jihadist organizations, who represented the third generation of mujahideen—those that had arrived in Afghanistan during the second phase of Arab Afghan immigration (1996–2001). Praise be to Allah that a number of them survived and spread across the globe.

The jihadist movement that arose in the 1960s and thrived in the 1970s and 1980s had great potential during the Taliban period in Afghanistan. Unfortunately, following the events of September 2001, the jihadist movement was utterly destroyed, bringing this period to an end. By the will of Allah, a new jihadist movement has arisen to confront the Zionist-Crusader campaigns. (Through my writings, I am participating in this new jihadist movement.) This period is marked by a U.S.-led war against terrorism. America has carried out a direct military invasion of Afghanistan, Iraq, and the Middle East. As a result, we have seen the emergence of new battlefields that will give us the opportunity to confront the Americans.

About Sheikh Osama bin Laden

Bin Laden has faced strong accusations and there were many writers and books filled with slanders. They said that there is a close relationship between the bin Laden family and Bush senior in the petroleum industry; particularly with one of Osama bin Laden's brothers. Moreover, it was said that bin Laden was working closely with Saudi intelligence in Peshawar and that he was preparing and organizing the Arabic jihad in Afghanistan at the behest and under the supervision of Saudi intelligence.

There were many allegations and lies in the media connecting bin Laden with Saudi intelligence as well as American intelligence. Some of the accusations went so far as to declare bin Laden an official agent of the CIA. They claim that he only turned against them when the Americans invaded Saudi Arabia and settled there after what they called the war and liberation of Kuwait. Some of them went even further and considered him still to be an agent when New York was struck. They claim it was done for the benefit of the Jews and that U.S. intelligence had prior information about the attack and chose not to prevent it in order to use the incident as a pretext to attack the Arab and Muslim countries and to destroy Afghanistan as well as invade Iraq!

They presented such evidence as that the Americans could not find Osama bin Laden and this was done intentionally! Many continue to go on with this unreasonable fiction. The reality and truth is simpler and does not need all these complications.

Sheikh Osama bin Laden made his way to Afghanistan after the Russian invasion to offer financial support to the Afghans. A trustworthy man told me in 1986 that bin Laden decided to settle in Afghanistan and fight in the Afghan jihad. There was a sheikh called Abdullah 'Azzam who had established a service agency in 1984. Osama bin Laden worked with the sheikh for a period of time. Subsequently, he separated from him and created his own organization, which he called al Qaida, in the beginning of 1988. He broke with the sheikh because of the increasing number of Arab mujahideen who came from Saudi Arabia and Yemen, who had a very close relationship with Osama bin Laden.

His move from Saudi Arabia to Afghanistan was public knowledge and legal. There was no opposition to the move from the Saudi government, because at that time there was agreement between the Saudi government and the U.S. government on matters concerning the Afghan jihad. This state of affairs continued until 1990.

When the Kuwait war broke out, Sheikh Osama reestablished al Qaida for jihadist goals both inside and outside Afghanistan. His views were shared by the other mujahideen organizations, which wanted to use Afghanistan as a training ground for members of al Qaida. This was being done by other groups as well, and like others, he worked toward a general goal, which was the creation of an Islamic state after Afghanistan's liberation. I myself worked intermittently in the field of military training in different al Qaida camps between 1988 and 1991. I also worked as a lecturer in the field of Islamic jurisprudence and politics. I also taught guerrilla tactics.

Through my work, I was involved with the founders and senior members in the Arab-Afghan jihad and know that at that time al Qaida had no interest in operations outside of Afghan territory. Sheikh Osama's only outside project was only directed at Yemen. In addition to that, Osama supported and funded other jihadist organizations and groups in many places. To the best of my knowledge and due to the fact that I was close to Sheikh bin Laden at the time, I believe that what I have said is the truth.

In 1991, I left Afghanistan and returned to my residence in Spain, cutting off my relationship with them. I did not have any contact with them again until 1996, when we all gathered at the invitation of the Taliban in Afghanistan. Sheikh Osama had by now traveled, with most of the senior members, to Sudan. There was no indication that they went there for jihad.

The field of Arab jihad in Afghanistan during the days of the Soviet jihad was complicated because of the enormous role of Saudi intelligence and different agencies in military and other aid. Many of their officials and representatives had a direct relationship with Arab services, which was headed by Sheikh Abdullah 'Azzam and Sheikh Osama bin Laden. Sheikh 'Azzam and Sheikh Osama, along with the other organizations, considered the relationship with the Saudis as useful work for the Afghan jihad. The mujahideen hid no secrets from Saudi or Pakistani intelligence. However, there were other jihadist groups who did not work with Saudi or Pakistani intelligence because they did not trust them. I was one of them. This was the case even though I was close to Sheikh bin Laden during that time.

It was said that the Americans had been training and supporting the Arab mujahideen from al Qaida. This is a blatant lie. The Arab jihad has been guided by the salafist ideology and did not deal with certain individuals in the Saudi government when they came to offer their help or open up camps, such as the military consul (Abu Mazin) at the Saudi embassy. If the mujahideen refused to deal with officials from the Saudi government, then how can it be said that they cooperated with foreigners and Americans?

I recognize that the media and various books that dealt with Sheikh al-Mujahideen Osama bin Laden did not give him credit for that period and afterward. They did not recognize or explain the timing of his ideological shift as well as the changes in his methods. Because they ignored this shift in his ideology and methods, bin Laden and al Qaida adopted a position against the United States of America.

There were two important factors that caused this situation, and I will mention them in order of importance:

1. Sheikh Osama had basically built al Qaida on the basis of the struggles of the Egyptian organization called al-Jihad al-Masri ("The Egyptian Jihad"), as well as on the training activities of other jihadists in various other places. Most of the mujahideen were not originally members of al Qaida. They came together for the sake of cooperation and mutual benefit. They committed themselves to their ideology and I was one of them. We were, in fact, so committed to our ideology that during training in our camps, we would fire shots at the portrait of King Fahd and other high princes in the Saudi family.

    Through their books, conversations, lectures, behavior, and so forth, the young al Qaida members made a profound impact on Sheikh Osama when he arrived in Afghanistan. Many young men from Saudi Arabia arrived in Afghanistan for jihad at the time. They had similar thoughts and feelings as Sheikh Osama and called their ideology the Saudi Islamic Awakening (al-Sahwa). This Islamic Awakening is a blend of the Muslim Brotherhood ideas and the official Wahabi school. I was very close to Sheikh Osama at this time, and he discussed this subject with me many times. Despite what many others thought, Sheikh Osama and the other Saudi mujahideen did not consider the Saudi government illegitimate. King Fahd and the al-Saud family are Muslims and legitimate under Islamic law. This is the case even though they are corrupt and decadent. They are respected by the official senior *ulema*. When the *ulema* issued a fatwa, the mujahideen, including Osama, would respect it. There was no similarity in thought between us (the foreign jihadist) and the brothers in Afghanistan. The only thing we shared in common was our religion and our dedication to the Afghan jihad. There were differences in opinion as well as in operation. Moreover, there were differences in jihadist thought and disagreements over political objectives. These differences among us were very sharp and clear. Sheikh Osama reflected on jihadist ideology and came to adopt it and soon became one of the most symbolic figures in jihadist ideology.

2. The position of the Saudi government and its administration as well as its official *ulema* during the Kuwait War [Persian Gulf War] and the presence of American troops on Saudi soil. What followed these events were major changes that revealed the magnitude of the disaster and the role of the great infidel that governed the Arab Peninsula. The religious establishment told lies about the state of affairs. Sheikh Osama, using his keen mind, recognized the reality of the situation. He understood the goals of the Americans in the region. His stay in Sudan (1992–96) gave him time to reflect on the situation. During this period, he shifted his view of the Saudi government from peaceful opposition through the media to more serious and stern opposition. He accused the government and the religious establishment of being liars.

When the Sudanese government expelled Sheikh Osama and he returned to Afghanistan in 1996, there was a group around him who were inspired by an ideology that consisted of an international opposition against the U.S. government and its allies. Sheikh Osama was affected by the jihadist wave, concluding that if he wanted to get rid of corrupt regimes in the Arab and Islamic world, including the Saudi regime, they would have to face America.

Sheikh Osama determined that if a strike was made at the American presence the Saudis would be forced to defend their American allies. Once this happened the Saudis would lose their legitimacy in the eyes of the people. When they lost their legitimacy, the religious establishment would have to defend the Saudi government. And when that happened, the religious establishment will also loose it legitimacy. Sheikh Osama chose this second strategy, and I think he was very accurate in that choice because it indicates that he understood the whole situation in Saudi Arabia and its religious, social, and political makeup.

Following the collapse of the Soviet Union, Sheikh Osama witnessed the downfall of the dictatorial states in the Warsaw Pact, such as the East German government, Romania, Poland, and others. He became convinced that if the United States collapsed, all of the corrupt regimes in the Arab and Muslim world would also collapse. For these reasons, he concentrated his efforts on the jihad against America. When people visited him, he would tell them that the mujahideen must fight against the "head of the snake," as he called America.

I came to Afghanistan in 1996, after bin Laden had been there for four to five months to conduct an interview with him for a BBC documentary concerning opposition to the Saudi government. Later, in May 1997, I interviewed him for CNN concerning Islamic studies. I sat with him [Osama] many times and came to share his beliefs. Because of this I returned to Afghanistan to reside there permanently during the Taliban period.

Throughout my four-year stay, I had many chances to visit Osama. I also visited many other friends who were working with him. When I was in his presence, I would tell his Arab and Persian guests what his beliefs were. I spoke about his views to the senior members of al-Sahwa and the young mujahideen. I think that the ideas Osama selected to launch the jihad against the Americans are the key to solving the problems in the Arab Peninsula and the whole region. Notwithstanding my opinion of the details of the operation and the organizational framework needed to carry out this operation, his ideas are basically correct.

As he laid out the reasons for jihad, Sheikh Osama became more and more committed to the struggle against America. Consequently, he established the tactics for this struggle. The media and various commentators have stated that Osama worked with the Americans during the Russian jihad and then turned against them. Such statements are false. The media attacks him because they are his enemies and despise him. These lies are built on spite and ignorance. The truth, in short, was that at the time Osama and the other Muslims had similar goals to the Americans. Their mutual goal was to drive the Russians out of Afghanistan. When the war ended, everyone became aware that the next enemy would be the remaining superpower. This superpower would establish a new global order and would invade Bilad al-Haramain [Land of the Two Holy Places, i.e., Saudi Arabia]. It will prepare a new crusader campaign to invade the Middle East. Bin Laden upheld his duty and declared jihad against this superpower, as did his network.

Other independent Islamic groups also declared jihad against the superpower. I was one of them. To make my point clear, I will offer a possible scenario: If the French or other Europeans, such as the Russians, or even China, were to help us in our jihad against America, which is a possibility, there will be shared interests and goals between us. However, if we overcome America, then it is likely that France, Russia, or China will in their turn invade our land. If this takes place, we will direct our jihad against them. However, if we find that they are cooperative and wish to be good neighbors, they will see that our religion has a peaceful side to it. Alas, I do not think this will be the case, because in all likelihood they will conspire against us at the appropriate time and circumstances.

Index

About the Editor

Having served more than a dozen years on active duty as an infantry officer and recently retired from the Army Reserve, Jim Lacey is a widely published analyst at the Institute for Defense Analyses in Washington, D.C., where he has written several studies on the war in Iraq and on the Global War on Terrorism. He also teaches graduate-level courses in military history and global issues at Johns Hopkins University. Lacey was an embedded journalist with *Time* magazine during the invasion of Iraq, where he traveled with the 101st Airborne Division. He has written extensively for many other magazines, and his opinion columns have been published in the *National Review*, *The Weekly Standard*, the *New York Post*, the *New York Sun*, and many other publications.

Lacey is the author of newly released *Takedown: The 3rd Infantry Division's Twenty-One Day Assault on Baghdad* (Naval Institute Press, 2006). Another book, *Fresh from the Fight: The Invasion and Occupation of Iraq: An Anthology of National War College Studies by American Combat Commanders*, will be released in summer 2007 by Zenith Press. Two other books, *Concluding Peace* (Cambridge University Press) and *Pershing* (Palgrave-Macmillan) are scheduled for publication in summer 2008.

The **Naval Institute Press** is the book-publishing arm of the U.S. Naval Institute, a private, nonprofit, membership society for sea service professionals and others who share an interest in naval and maritime affairs. Established in 1873 at the U.S. Naval Academy in Annapolis, Maryland, where its offices remain today, the Naval Institute has members worldwide.

Members of the Naval Institute support the education programs of the society and receive the influential monthly magazine *Proceedings* or the colorful bimonthly magazine *Naval History* and discounts on fine nautical prints and on ship and aircraft photos. They also have access to the transcripts of the Institute's Oral History Program and get discounted admission to any of the Institute-sponsored seminars offered around the country.

The Naval Institute's book-publishing program, begun in 1898 with basic guides to naval practices, has broadened its scope to include books of more general interest. Now the Naval Institute Press publishes about seventy titles each year, ranging from how-to books on boating and navigation to battle histories, biographies, ship and aircraft guides, and novels. Institute members receive significant discounts on the Press's more than eight hundred books in print.

Full-time students are eligible for special half-price membership rates. Life memberships are also available.

For a free catalog describing Naval Institute Press books currently available, and for further information about joining the U.S. Naval Institute, please write to:

Member Services
U.S. Naval Institute
291 Wood Road
Annapolis, MD 21402-5034
Telephone: (800) 233-8764
Fax: (410) 571-1703
Web address: www.usni.org